101
Creati...

Sol...
...or before the last date shown below.

Techniques
The Handbook of New Ideas
for Business
Revised Edition

James M. Higgins

Cornell Professor of Innovation Management
Crummer Graduate School of Business
Rollins College
and President of
James M. Higgins & Associates Inc.

THE NEW
MANAGEMENT
PUBLISHING COMPANY

1960 Forrest Road
Winter Park, FL 32789 USA

PRODUCTION MANAGER: Susan Novotny

DEVELOPMENTAL EDITOR: Carolyn D. Smith

ILLUSTRATOR: Keri Caffrey

WORD PROCESSOR: Susan Crabill

New Management Publishing Company, Inc.
1960 Forrest Road
Winter Park, Florida 32789
nmpc@aol.com or phone 407-647-5344, or fax 407-647-5575

The following is Publisher's Cataloging-in-Publication Data for the 1st Edition. None is required for this Revised Edition. Revised edition information is noted.
Higgins, James M.
101 Creative Problem Solving Techniques: The Handbook of New Ideas for Business/James M. Higgins.
p. cm.
Includes bibliographical references and index.

ISBN 1-883629-05-5 (Revised Edition, 10 character)
ISBN 978-1-883629-05-2 (Revised Edition, 13 character)
1. Problem solving. 2. Organizational change. I. Title. II. Title: One hundred and one creative problem solving techniques.

HD30.29.H54 1994 (1st Edition)
658.4'063
QBI93-22664   93-8702
                                                  P-CIP

Printing   123456789

This book is dedicated to my associate Susan Novotny for her dedication to this and our other projects, for her talent in integrating so many complex facets of our various projects, and for her good cheer, especially at crunch time..

PREFACE

Businesses and their managers, professional staff, team leaders, and other employees are confronted with a host of challenges in this decade of the 21st century. Change is occurring at an accelerating rate. The number and strength of competitors is increasing dramatically. Business and life are globalizing even more than they have in the recent past. New technologies are being introduced at a rapid pace. The composition of the workforce is increasingly diverse, not just in terms of factors such as gender, age, and ethnicity, but also factors such as values and beliefs as well. There is a scarcity of certain resources, including energy and highly skilled workers. There is a transformation occurring from an industrial to a knowledge based society. Economic and market conditions are increasingly unstable, especially on a global basis. Constituents are more demanding. The entire business environment is becoming more complex. And finally, global warming is beginning to have significant impacts on our lives and on the conduct of business.

To meet these challenges and to take advantage of the opportunities they create, businesses are embracing creative problem solving and innovation as never before. To achieve effective and efficient levels of creative problem solving and the innovation which results, an organization must improve the creativity of its work groups and individuals, and it must create an organizational context which promotes innovation.

One of the key ways in which individuals and groups can improve their creativity is through learning creativity techniques, processes that take advantage of innate intuitive and creative abilities and channel these abilities to create new or enhanced products or services, or create more effective and efficient organizational processes. This book describes the basic creative problem solving (CPS) model and then describes 101 techniques for unleashing individual and group creativity. These techniques are presented by their stage in the CPS process.

Managers, professionals, team leaders, and any other employee interested in improving his or her job performance or that of the work group, or for that matter, the entire company, will find this book beneficial. This book is readily useable in company training programs. Organizational creativity training programs have grown rapidly in recent months, and this book is designed to meet the needs of such programs. Additional training materials are also available. And, individuals wishing to give themselves a skill set that most other people have not developed are also well served by this book.

Two other books by this same author are also available from this publisher. Together these three books form a trilogy on creativity and innovation. *Escape from the Maze: Increasing Individual and Group Creativity* is like this book, a book about creativity. *Innovate or Evaporate: Test and Improve Your Organization's IQ—Its Innovation Quotient* describes how an organization can help foster creativity and turn that creativity into innovation, the innovation necessary for organizational survival and prosperity in this century. An order form for these books can be found at the end of this book.

THANKS

No book is the work of the author alone. I want to thank several people for their critical inputs into this book. First, Susan Novotny artfully managed the operations process from beginning to end. And, as with the first edition, the art of Keri Caffrey creatively illustrates the creativity being described. Carolyn Smith did a superb job of much of the developmental editing of the original manuscript. My business reviewers have provided important insights into the perspectives of the book. In addition, the Crummer Graduate School of Business is a special place in the academic universe where an applications orientation and creative freedom are the orders of the day rather than the exception. I therefore want to thank Dean Craig McAllaster for his support of this project, and the deans who preceded him. And finally, my wife, Susan, has provided tremendous support during this lengthy writing and publication process.

TABLE OF CONTENTS

Chapter 1
INNOVATE OR EVAPORATE

Chapter 2
THE CREATIVE PROBLEM
SOLVING PROCESS

Chapter 3
CREATIVE TECHNIQUES FOR ANALYZING THE ENVIRONMENT, RECOGNIZING & IDENTIFYING PROBLEMS, AND MAKING ASSUMPTIONS

Chapter 4
INDIVIDUAL TECHNIQUES FOR
GENERATING ALTERNATIVES

Chapter 5
GROUP TECHNIQUES FOR
GENERATING ALTERNATIVES

Chapter 6
CREATIVE TECHNIQUES FOR CHOOSING AMONG THE ALTERNATIVES, IMPLEMENTATION, AND CONTROL

Chapter 7
USING THE TECHNIQUES

INNOVATE OR EVAPORATE

Increasingly, the new core competence is creativity.
— *Bruce Nussbaum*
Business week

When Whirlpool found itself mired in an industry characterized as "a sea of white appliances," where little differentiated any competitor's products, it turned to product innovation as the means of becoming a dominant player in its industry. It did so within just five years by first making innovation its strategy and then by creating the right kind of organizational environment to nourish creativity and innovation. For example, among the many actions it took, Whirlpool trained its employees to use creativity tools and techniques, provided the proper motivation to be creative and innovative, encouraged responsible risk taking, and provided recognition for successful creativity and innovation.[1]

When Cirque du Soleil founders Guy Laliberte´ and Daniel Gauthier began their version of the circus, they set out to create something that would totally redefine the circus industry. They created a circus that was more an artistic vision than a series of circus performances. Today, Cirque isn't just one circus, there are five traveling shows and four shows with permanent locations, each a series of unique experiences and themes. Each starts with the basic circus performers, for example, trapeze artists, clowns, and contortionists, and their equipment (no animal acts) and then dresses the performers in surreal costumes, surrounds them with spectacular sets, uses dazzling stagecraft and nonstop new age music, and ties it altogether with a vague theme, such as a tribute to a nomadic soul,' at its Varekai show. Cirque is all about innovation. True, the owners made sound business decisions and hired quality staff, but at the core of the company is continuous creativity and innovation. For their managers' annual performance reviews, this question is always asked, "What did you innovate this year?[2]

When Intel's chief competitor for PC chips, AMD, got tired of being bested by Intel seemingly at every turn when it was an Intel imitator, CEO Jesus Ruiz steered the company toward both product and process innovation. The company launched a series of new microprocessors that proved popular with corporate clients, smoothly launched new manufacturing processes, and pushed new chip designs that had exceedingly high demand. AMD innovated its way into besting Intel at its own game—innovation—for the first time in AMD's history.[3]

And when Sidney Frank decided to turn one of his brands, Grey Goose Vodka into the premier vodka brand, he used innovative marketing to achieve this end. Vodka is basically a commodity, so the innovation comes in convincing the consumer otherwise. Sidney Frank's strategy was to give the vodka a high price, make it a fixture at ritzy events, and hawk it as the world's best-tasting vodka after it won a taste award in 1998. This innovative marketing strategy worked so well that Sidney eventually sold Grey Goose to Bacardi Ltd. for more than $2 billion.[4]

Surviving and prospering in business have never been easy. There are always problems to be solved and opportunities to be taken advantage of. But during the next few years, from now through the foreseeable future, business organizations, their managers, and their other employees will be confronted with a number of strategic challenges unmatched in business history.

The primary challenges are these.[5]

1. Every facet of business is changing at an accelerating rate.
2. Competition is increasing.
3. Business, already global, is becoming increasingly even more global in scope.
4. New technologies are being introduced at a breathtaking rate.
5. The composition of the work force is changing, as are its members' values and expectations.
6. There are increasing shortages of resources ranging from water to skilled employees.
7. The U.S. economy is being transformed from an industrial economy to one based on knowledge and information.
8. Market and economic conditions throughout the world are extremely unstable.
9. Constituents, such as shareholders, government and environmentalists, are making greater demands on the organization.
10. Not only is the business environment changing rapidly, but it is becoming much more complex.
11. Global warming is about to present a whole new and different set of challenges, not just to business, but to everyone on the planet.

As a consequence of these challenges, every facet of business, from overall strategy to daily operations, is full of new problems and opportunities. And the task of just "doing business" remains. This in itself is difficult enough without all of these additional burdens. How can a business or any part of it survive and prosper in the face of such challenges?

Virtually every leading authority on business, including Fortune 500 CEOs, researchers, and consultants, agree that there is one primary way firms can best cope with all of the challenges confronting them in the 21st Century. *By being creative and innovative!*[6] Whirlpool, Cirque du Soleil, AMD and Grey Goose all did so in order to survive and prosper. The message is clear, *"Innovate or evaporate!"*

CREATIVITY AND INNOVATION

Something new is said to be **original**. **Creativity** is the process of generating something new, something original that has value to an individual, a group, an organization, an industry, or a

society.[7] There are millions of original ideas conceptualized every day, but many do not have any or much value and hence are not creations. **A creation** is something original that has value. Something is said to be **creative** if it is new and has value. For example, a new cell phone design might be labeled creative because it is so cool looking. Or, an accounting process idea might be called creative because it could save a company money.

People who are consistently turning out creative ideas are sometimes referred to as **creatives**. Among those often designated as creatives are artists, musicians, authors, successful ad generators, product designers, and research and development scientists, engineers and technicians. This book describes 101 techniques for increasing creativity—the first step in achieving innovation. These techniques can help everyone, including creatives, to be more creative.

Innovation results from and builds on creativity. **Innovation** is the process of taking a creation and turning it into something that has *significant* value to an individual, a group, an organization, an industry, or a society. **An innovation** is a creation that has *significant* value to at least one of these entities. The primary difference between something being creative and something being innovative is the level of significance of the value—the greater the value of the creation, the more likely that it is also an innovation. **Innovation** is also often described as the process of taking an invention (a creation) and making it profitable through successful application.

4

Innovation is all about having an impact. For a creation to be an innovation it must have a substantial impact. In business that impact is primarily financial in nature—it's about making money. Businesses seek to create original ideas and concepts that will end up as innovations— impactful new or enhanced products or services; new or enhanced processes that significantly increase productivity; or highly innovative marketing efforts or management and leadership actions or other types of innovation that produce superior results. PDA-cell phone combinations such as Blackberry and Treo are product innovations. Enterprise resource planning systems such as those provided by SAP are process innovations. Advertising products and services over the Web is a marketing innovation. Level 5 leadership is a leadership style innovation identified by Jim Collins.

An increasingly critical part of innovating new or enhanced products and services is design. The "power of design" not only includes the design of the physical product or of the service experience, but the packaging of the product or service, or the accoutrements of the experience.[8] With products and services having so many similar features, it is the design of the product or the customer experience that often differentiates the successful product or service from its competitors.

Not-for-profit organizations can also innovate and create innovations, but typically their innovations are not products or services that are sold, but rather they are creations that have significant impact in terms of cutting costs, improving services, or perhaps raising funds.

To be able to distinguish among what is original, creative, and innovative is important. First, you and your organization need to know how to generate creative ideas and then you both must be able to tell whether the ideas you generate are creative or merely original. Original ideas just aren't enough. Secondly, to be innovative you and your organization need to go beyond merely being creative. You and your organization need to know whether the ideas you generate have the potential for significant value—the potential to become innovations. Finally, you and your organization must know how to turn creations into innovations.

Creativity—The Springboard To Innovation

Earlier creativity was defined as a process. But creativity is also something else. *Creativity is a skill—the skill of generating something new, something original that has value to an individual, a group, an organization, an industry, or a society—the new key word in this definition is* **skill***. Creativity is not something mystical, available only to a few. Every person possesses an innate capacity for creativity, and the means to unleash it can be learned by anyone.* But the development of this capacity into a skill has been thwarted, for the most part by teachers and bosses who provide and enforce rules about what is acceptable behavior. Studies show that anywhere from 70% to 90% of creativity potential is lost after just one year of school, between ages 6 and 7.[9] Because only a few, carefully structured behaviors are allowed at school and at work, and creativity is usually not one of them, creativity is stifled. Therefore, *you* must act to develop your creativity skill; *you* must work to unleash your creative capacity; *you* must fulfill your untapped potential.

Learning creativity techniques such as those described in this book is the quickest and surest way to increasing your untapped creativity potential. Learning and using these techniques constitute just one of the nine steps to creativity discussed in another book I have written, *Escape from the Maze: Nine Steps to Personal Creativity*.[10] But based on my experience as a consultant, educator and researcher, I believe that creativity techniques offer the quickest and most impactful means of achieving higher levels of creativity—the biggest bang for the buck. So I wrote this book before I wrote *Escape from the Maze*, and the other book in my innovation trilogy, *Innovate or Evaporate*,[11] which describes the environment of an innovative organization, what I label as the innovative organizational context.

Creativity can be incremental, occurring in a series of small progressive steps such as the lengthy, painstaking research that led to the development of polio vaccine. Conversely, creativity can involve giant leaps of progress in which many links in the evolutionary chain of concepts are hurdled by a single effort. The invention of cell phones was a giant leap in technology at the time that they were

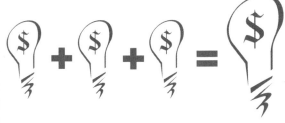

introduced, and they had a hugely significant impact on numerous societies around the globe. Then when all of the incremental improvements began—a merger with the PDA, digital cameras, video, and games, the cell phone innovation became even more impactful. This product is both an example of big bang innovation, and also of how continuous, incremental improvements also result in innovation.

The product of the creative effort need not be a tangible physical object. It may be an idea, an association of facts, an insight, or a more effective or efficient process as well as a new or enhanced product or service. Each of these, when fully expressed and functioning, has value.

For an organization, one of the critical steps in achieving innovation is developing the creative problem-solving skills of its human resources—its managers, professionals, and other employees. This book is designed to help you and/or your organization to develop those skills. The remaining chapters in this book present 101 techniques or processes for making problem solving more creative. Many managers, professional staff and other employees that I know or know of, would never solve problems individually or in groups/teams without using these techniques.

THE INNOVATION EQUATION

The ultimate business purpose of creativity is to achieve innovation. To better understand the relationships between creativity and innovation in organizations, it is useful to think in terms of the "Innovation Equation." Figure 1.1 presents this equation and its subparts in more detail.

As seen in Figure 1.1, the innovation equation is:

$$C \text{ (X) } IOC \text{ (X) } SSE = I.$$

In words, this equation says:
Creativity (C)
occurring in an (X)
Innovative **O**rganizational **C**ontext (IOC)
within a (X)
Supportive **S**ocietal **E**nvironment (SSE)
results in (=)
Innovation (I).

This equation is mulplicative. That is, if an organization is only half as good at creativity as it should be, and has only half as good of an innovative organizational context as it should, and has only half the societal support that it should have, then it will be only one-eighth as good at innovation as it should be.

Figure 1.1 The Innovation Equation

C	(X)	IOC	(X)	SSE	=	I
CREATIVITY		INNOVATIVE ORGANIZATIONAL CONTEXT		SUPPORTIVE SOCIETAL ENVIRONMENT		INNOVATION
		Occuring In An		Within A		Results In
1. Individual Creativity · Individual Techniques · CPS Process 2. Group/Team Creativity · Group Techniques · CPS Process		1. Strategy/Purposes 2. Structure 3. Systems/Processes 4. Style 5. Staff 6. reSources 7. Shared Values		1. Supportive Govt. Policies, Taxes 2. Innovation Viewed as Positive 3. Society Approves Entrepreneurship 4. Positive View of Achievement 5. Major Research Universities 6. Strong Public Education 7. Cluster of Related Businesses 8. Access to Capital		1. Product/Service 2. Process 3. Marketing 4. Management 5. Numerous Other Types of Innovation

Now let's examine the parts of this equation in more detail.

Creativity

Figure 1.1 reveals that there are two primary types of creativity—individual and group/team creativity. The figure also indicates that there are creativity techniques that are primarily used by individuals and that there are creativity techniques that are primarily used by groups and teams. Chapter 4 describes those solution generating creativity techniques that are primarily used by individuals, while Chapter 5 describes those that are primarily used by groups. An important point though is that almost all individual techniques can be used by groups, and vice versa for group techniques. So the designations are used only to show who uses these techniques the most and thus where you might look first as an individual or as a group/team member when trying to find a creativity technique to use.

But don't forget to check both chapters when seeking solution generation techniques. For example, mind mapping is listed in Chapter 4 as an individual technique, but it is very often used by groups and teams to discover great new ideas. I once participated in a team facilitation wherein 15 team members using three facilitators filled three wall boards 6' high by 9' wide with mind mapping ideas related to transforming organizational technology in just 45 minutes.

Figure 1.1 also indicates that the Creative Problem Solving (CPS) Process (discussed in Chapter 2) applies to both individual and group/team creativity efforts. The Creative Problem Solving process model is similar to most problem solving models with which you are probably familiar, except that creativity is stressed in each of the eight stages: analyzing the environment, recognizing a problem, identifying the problem, making assumptions, generating alternatives, choosing among alternatives, implementing the choices made and controlling for results. Creativity, if it has been referred to at all in most problem solving models, is usually only discussed in the generating alternatives stage. Creativity techniques exist for all eight stages.

Occurring In An Innovative Organizational Context

Figure 1.1 also describes the primary areas involved in achieving an innovative organizational context. These are the organization's strategy and purposes, organizational structure, systems and processes, leadership style, staff situations, the resources available and their allocation, and the organization's shared values.

Figure 1.2 portrays the relationships among these seven factors, and introduces an eighth and resulting factor—strategic performance. The visual premise of this model is that all the arrows should be pointed in the same direction. That means that the actions taken or policies established for each contextual S must support the achievement desired in the 8th S, Strategic Performance. Pragmatically this means that first strategic objectives are determined, a strategy is formulated to achieve those objectives, and the remaining six contextual Ss must all be aligned with those objectives and that strategy. If the seven contextual Ss are aligned, then strategic performance should be achieved.

If an organization or group/team is not acting to provide an innovative organizational context—that is, if it is not providing a supportive and motivating environment for innovation, then the level of innovation obtained will be insufficient to achieve organizational objectives. An organization will not have the products and services it needs to survive and prosper in the market place and it won't be able to offer these at the right price point (unless it also has innovative processes). Regardless of your creative talents, regardless of however great your knowledge or creativity skills, you will not be able to create many innovations if you are not functioning in a favorable situation. If the organization's context does not support and even require innovation, innovation is unlikely.

Figure 1.2 The Eight Ss of Innovation

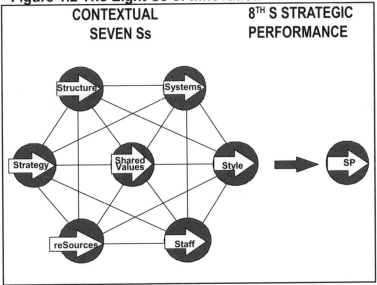

CONTEXTUAL
SEVEN Ss

8TH S STRATEGIC
PERFORMANCE

Examples of some of the many important actions to take to achieve an innovative organizational context include:

1. Strategy and Purposes: require managers to have objectives for innovation; have a strategy for innovation.
2. Structure: have cross functional and customer/supplier new product/service development teams; use alliances to obtain innovations.
3. Systems and Processes: have reward systems for creativity and innovation; have formal idea assessment systems.
4. Style (Leadership): encourage risk taking; use special approaches in managing highly creative personnel.
5. Staff: have innovation champions; train people in the use of creativity techniques; and use these techniques in everyday problem solving.
6. reSources: invest heavily, but appropriately in R&D; practice knowledge management and organizational learning.
7. Shared Values: possess a shared value that this is an innovative organization; manage organizational culture to make it congruent with innovation.

Within A Supportive Societal Environment

Research by Michael E. Porter, a renowned business strategy researcher and consultant, and several others has clearly demonstrated what we have long suspected—it is easier to innovate in some geographic locations than others.[12] This is because these places have more of the necessary supportive environmental factors that lead to successful innovation than do other locations. For example, it is easier to innovate in Silicon Valley, California, than it is to innovate in Jackson, Mississippi. Similarly it is easier to innovate in Denmark than in Germany, in Singapore than in Japan, in Boston than in Paris. There are several factors that constitute a supportive societal environment. Some of these are a supportive govern- ment in terms of policies and economic factors such as taxes, a positive view of innovation by the society, an acceptance of entrepreneurs as being vital contributors, a positive view of achievement, major research universities, and an excellent public education system.[13] Clusters of related businesses and access to capital are also critical factors.

For example, Silicon Valley has a world class research and technology leading university, and it has several clusters of related technology businesses that bring together idea people and a number of sources of venture capital. It also possesses several of the other characteristics. Jackson, Mississippi does not possess these same attributes.

Results In Innovation

As shown in Figure 1.2, the 8th S is Strategic Performance. When the 8 S's model is applied to innovation in businesses, strategic performance focuses on the contributions of successful new or enhanced products/services and processes to the organization's bottom line—its profit. There are numerous types of innova- tion—marketing innovation, finance innovation, operations innovation, supply chain innovation, management innovation, research and development innovation, and so on. But all types of innovation can be classified as either product/service or process innovation. The definition of the term "successful" when applied to innovation varies by organization but generally successful innovation would significantly increase profits for the organization. Several metrics exist for measuring innovation success—everything from return on investment in a new product or service to the number of new products or services launched in a year.

How do you determine what has potentially significant value? Sometimes by analysis. Sometimes by intuition. Value is relative, both to the value systems of the evaluator and to the time during which the creation occurs. For example, twelve Hollywood studios turned down the "Star Wars" movie concept. Finally Twentieth Century Fox agreed to take the risk and made the most financially successful movie series of all time. Similarly, some inventors and their investors offered to sell a new idea to IBM, General Motors, Du Pont, and several other major firms and were turned down by all of them. Finally, they decided to build and market the product themselves and became multimillionaires. The process was photocopying. The company became Xerox.[14]

Even successful entrepreneurs may misjudge the value of a creation and, hence its potential to become an innovation. Victor Kiam, of Remington Razor fame, was once offered the patent to Velcro for $25,000; he turned it down, believing it had no future. Sales of Velcro products now amount to well over several billion dollars annually.[15] Chapter 6, discusses some ways for determining whether a product is innovative or not.

Finally, a business does not have to create something in order to turn it into an innovation. It can acquire a creation and then turn it into an innovation. For example, it is well known that Bill Gates paid $50,000 for the DOS operating system, which he has turned into a personal wealth of over $40 billion. Before he acquired it, this PC operating system was languishing. For years, the Japanese have taken products created in the U.S., improved them through product enhancement innovation, made them less expensive through process innovation, and turned them into innovations in our own country. Now the Koreans and Chinese are following precisely the same strategy while building their innovation capacities. Furthermore, many companies now acquire someone else's inventions or services and market them in more impactful ways than the inventors or creators might have been able to. Instead of research and development, these firms practice search (searching for product/ services, acquisitions, mergers, or alliances) and development.

CREATIVITY, INNOVATION, AND COMPETITIVENESS

All organizations compete based on some combination of two primary factors:

1. The relative differentiation of their products and/or services from those of their competitors, and
2. The relative low-cost of their products compared to those of their competitors.

Figure 1.3 provides a model created by William K. Hall depicting how these two factors combine to enable a firm to be competitive.[16] The following paragraphs discuss this model beginning with competitive power alleys.

Hall's research indicates that firms that have a very high degree of differentiation relative to that of their competitors, or a very low cost position relative to that of their competitors, operate within competitive power alleys. For example, the Chrysler 300C automobile captured a strong (high) differentiation position in the time period of 2004-2006. Note that it also possessed a mid-level relative low-cost so that it would be positioned on Hall's model approximately as indicated in Figure 1.3. Design played an important role in this car's success. The look of the car gave it a significant differentiation from competitors' cars in the same price and model category. But the Chrysler 300C also had many important additional features, including a hemi-engine, which added to its differentiation. In contrast, most companies find their products in the zone of

14

competitive battle rather than in one power alley or another. For example, the Ford Expedition in that same time frame would be placed approximately in the area shown in Figure 1.3, reflecting moderate level differentiation and moderate level relative low cost. Eventually, many products end up in the section, "Losing Competitiveness." The Chevrolet Camaro was dis-

Figure 1.3 Hall's Competitiveness Model

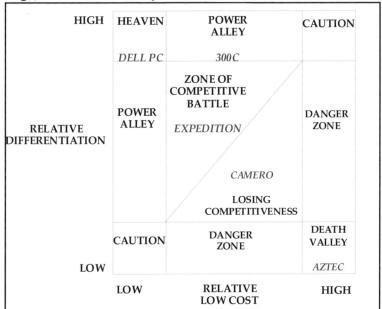

continued in 2002 because GM felt it had lost its competitiveness. And for some products, Death Valley is where they start as products. The Pontiac Aztec, for example, was stylistically differentiated but not in a positive way, and had little if any relative low cost. The Hall model can be used for products or services, product or service lines, strategic business units, or for whole companies. The higher the differentiation and the lower the relative costs, the higher the margins the company will garner for a particular product. The other sections of the model are self-explanatory.

The Hall model links directly to creativity and innovation because most of the time product/service innovation provides differentiation and most of the time process innovation provides relative low cost. Sometimes process innovation leads to differentiation and vice versa. For example, in seeking to be the swiftest deliverer of PCs—a differentiation factor—Dell eliminated a number of parts from the PC and redesigned processes to shorten the assembly time. In so doing, they also provided their PCs with a very low relative delivered cost, putting their PC product line in the Garden of Eden. Sometimes relative low costs are not the result of innovation. For example, almost all products imported into the U.S. from China in the first decade of the 21st century enjoyed a relative low cost position due primarily to lower wage rates in that country than in the U.S.

However, insufficient innovation is generally considered to be the primary cause of a lack of competitiveness in most product markets. Similarly, increased innovation is the most often recommended solution to the problem of ailing competitiveness especially for improving global competetiveness.[17]

Unfortunately, from the perspective of U.S. based firms, firms in already highly competitive regions or countries such as those in the European Union, China, India, and Japan, are becoming more proficient in the skills of creativity and innovation. Even more unfortunately for U.S. based firms is the fact these skills are often taught to these foreign firms by U.S. based firms themselves. Thus these firms have begun to erode U.S. based firms' global lead in innovation.[18] Hence, the abilities to create and to innovate are growing ever more critical to U.S. based firms as well as to firms around the globe.

But innovation isn't just about competitiveness, in solving their other strategic challenges and in "doing business" every day, firms will not be as effective or efficient as they should be if they cannot be creative and innovative. Solving problems and pursuing opportunities requires solutions, many of which may be unique to the specific situation. Research studies in the past few years have consistently shown over and over that creativity and innovation are fundamental to the survival and prosperity of business organizations. Shareholder value, growth and return on investment are all higher for highly innovative firms than for much less innovative firms. These studies also show that employees benefit as well from working in innovative firms because typically the cultures of innovative organizations have employment practices that result in high levels of employee job satisfaction.[19]

Leading creativity and innovation are increasingly critical leader-manager skills. As we move further into the 21st century, two things are becoming increasingly clear. First that the future will be one of continuing rapid innovation; and second that innovation will be the key to long term business growth and success.

Finally, because of the strategic challenges, but especially because competition is so fierce, companies must continuously innovate in order to remain competitive. To do so requires high level creativity skills and innovation skills. Chapter 2 will begin your introduction to those creativity skills.

CREATIVITY AND INNOVATION AT P&G

A good place to start when creativity and innovation are needed is with the customer. It isn't always the best place to start, especially in technology businesses, because the customer may not know what's possible or what's coming down the technology pipeline. But one thing is for sure, the customer will eventually make the buying decision so it never hurts to find out what the customer needs and then create and innovate to satisfy those needs.

That's precisely what Alan. G. Lafley, CEO of Procter and Gamble, did when he turned around the fortunes of this consumer products giant. Lafly employed a three pronged strategy: find out what women want, focus on design, and pursue (what can only be called quiet) innovation. Drawing on his numerous years of experience at P&G, Lafley wanted to make sure P&G knew what its customers wanted. Using focus groups, lengthy observations of women at work at home and in the lab, interviews in grocery stores, and numerous customer surveys produced some interesting results. Lafley summarized their findings for a group of P&G executives in Caracas as follows, "We discovered that women don't care about our technology and they couldn't care less what machine a product is made on. They want to hear that we understand them."

Making the customer experience as positive as possible thus became a focal point of P&G products. And having learned the power of design from his four years of experience running P&G's Asian operation from Japan, Lafley recognized that product and packaging designs were critical components of that experience. He thus steered the firm towards creative and innovative designs. Finally, he knew that product function was a key ingredient of the customer experience and thus led the organization to pursue more product enhancements as well as new products. Lafley recognized that P&G needed improved products not just new ones. The results speak for themselves. In his five years as CEO, the company has experienced an average of 17% increase in earnings and P&G's stock price has doubled.

Sources: Sarah Ellison, "Focus Group—P&G Chief's Turnaround Recipe: Find Out What Women Want," *Wall Street Journal* (June 1, 2005), pp. Al, A16; Jennifer Reingold, "What P&G Knows About the Power of Design," *Fast Company* (June 2004), pp. 56, 57.

REFERENCES

[1] Ann Pomery, "Cooking Up Innovation," *HR Magazine* (November 2004), pp. 46-50.

[2] W. Chan Kim, Renee Mauborgne, "Blue Ocean Strategy," *Harvard Business Review* (October 2004), p. 76; Geoff Keighley, "The Phastasmagoria Factory," *Fast Company* (January/February 2004), pp. 103-107.

[3] Cliff Edwards, "Suddenly, It's AMD Inside," *Business Week* (September 20, 2004), pp. 32-35.

[4] Diane Brady, "The Wily Fox Behind Grey Goose," *Business Week* (September 20, 2004), pp. 71, 73.

[5] Cait Murphy, "How the World Will Work: The Next 75 Years," *Fortune* (September 2005) Pullout, unnumbered; Editors, "Outlook 2005" *The Futurist* (November-December 2004), pp. 29-40; Susan Joy Hassol, ACIA, *Impacts of a Warming Artic: Artic Climate Impact Assessment* (Cambridge: Cambridge University Press, 2004), http://www.acia.uaf.edu; David Pearce Snyder, "Five Meta-Trends Changing the World," *The Futurist* (July/August 2004), pp. 22-27; Genaro C. Armas, "U. S. Population Surges on Growth of Hispanics, Asians," Associated Press, *Orlando Sentinel* (June 15, 2004), p. A4; Victor Mallet, "Power Hungry: Asia's Surging Energy Demand Reverberates around the World," *Financial Times* (May 12, 2004), p. 13; Andy Reinhardt, Hiroko Tashior, and Ben Elgin, "The Camera Phone Revolution," *Business Week* (April 12, 2004), p. 52; Peronet Despeignes, "Report: Medicare to Go Broke by 2019," *USA Today* (March 24, 2004), p. 7A; Ayako Doi, "From Boom to Bust," *Financial Times* (March 21, 2004), pp. W1, 2; Greg Ip, "The Gap in Wages is Growing Again for U. S. Workers," *Wall Street Journal*," (January 23, 2004), pp. A1, A4; Scott Kirsner, "5 Technologies that Will Change the World," *Fast Company* (September 2003), pp. 93-100; "The Future of Technolgoy," *Business Week* (August 18-25), entire issue; Caroline Louise Cole, et. al, "25 Trends that Will Change the Way You Do Business," *Workforce* (June 2003), pp. 43-56; Marvin J. Cetron and Own Davies, "Trends Shaping the Future: Technological, Workplace, Management, and Institutional Trends," *The Futurist* (March-April 2003), pp. 30-43; Marvin J. Cetron and Own Davies, "Trends Shaping the Future: Economic, Societal, and Environmental Trends, *The Futurist* (January-February 2003), pp. 27-42; Peter Drucker, *Management Challenges for the 21st Century* (New York: Harper Business, 2001).

[6] Bruce Nussbuam, "Get Creative," *Business Week* (August 1, 2005), pp. 60-68. Robert D. Hof, "Building an Idea Factory," *Business Week* (October 11, 2004), pp. 194-200; "Special Report—The Innovation Economy," *Business Week* (October 11, 2004), throughout.

[7] John G. Young, "What is Creativity?" *The Journal of Creative Behavior* (1985, 2nd Quarter), pp. 77-87.

[8] Various authors, "The Masters of Design" *Fast Company* (June 2005), entire issue devoted to design and 20 masters of design; Bruce Nussbaum, "The Power of Design: IDEO Redefined Good Design by Creating Experiences, not Just Products; Now It's Changing the Way Companies Innovate," *Business Week* (May 17, 2004), pp. 88-99.

[9] George Land, "Creativity of the Heart," (Santa Barbara, California: Innovative Thinking Convergence 95) April 12, 1995; also see Emily T. Smith, "Mix Skepticism, Humor, a Rocky Childhood—and Pronto! Creativity" *Business Week* (September 30, 1985), p. 45; Emily T. Smith, Stephanie Yanchinski, Margaret Sabin, and Pam Ellis Simmons, "Are You Creative? Research Shows Creativity Can be Taught—and Companies Are Listening," *Business Week* (September 3, 1985), pp. 80-84.

[10] James M. Higgins, *Escape from the Maze: Nine Steps to Personal Creativity* (Winter Park, FL: New Management Publishing Company, 1997).

[11] James M. Higgins, *Innovate or Evaporate: Test and Improve Your Organization's IQ, Its Innovation Quotient* (Winter Park, FL: The New Management Publishing Company, 1995).

[12] Michael E. Porter, "The Economic Performance of Regions," *Regional Studies* (August-October, 2003), pp. 549-578.

[13] Ted Abernathy, "Breathing New Life Into NC's Research Triangle," *World Trade* (June 2004), pp. 42-46; Jeffrey L. Furman, Michael E Porter, Scott Stern, "The Determinants of National Innovative Capacity," *Research Policy* (August 2002), pp. 899-933. This study uses patents over time as the measure of innovation.

[14] Chester Carlson—Xerography," Xerox Internal Documents; "A Profile in Entrepreneurship," a special advertising session, *Inc.* (July 1988), pp. 109, 110.

[15] Victor Kiam, speech to the Roy E. Crummer Graduate School of Business, Rollins College, Winter Park, FL (October 28, 1985).

[16] William K. Hall, "Surivival Strategies in a Hostile Environment," *Harvard Business Review* (September-October, 1980), pp. 73-86.

[17] Bruce Nussbaum, "Where Are the Jobs?" *Business Week* (March 22, 2004), pp. 36-46; Carly Fiorina, "Be Creative, Not Protectionist,: *Wall Street Journal* (February 13, 2004), p. A 12.

[18] Pete Engardio, Bruce Einhorn, Manjeet Kripalani, and Andy Reinhardt, "Outsourcing Innovation," *Business Week* (March 21, 2005), pp. 84-96.

[19] W. Chan Kim and Renée Mauborgne, op, cit.; "Price-Waterhouse-Coopers: Innovation 2000 Study," (London: Price-Waterhouse, Coopers, 2000);
Gary Hamel, "Killer Strategies that Make Shareholders Rich," *Fortune* (June 23, 1997), pp. 70-84; Editor, "Short Takes: Two Strategies for Growth, *Journal of Business Strategy*, (July-August, 1997), pp. 3,4 reporting on a study done by Michael A. May of Andersen Consulting; Charles E. Lucier and Amy Asin, "Toward A New Theory of Growth," *Strategy & Business* (Winter 1996), pp. 10-16; "Ed Michaels and Phil Humann, "Emerging Best Practices in Leading and Organizing for Growth," (Strategic Leadership Forum: Atlanta, GA:, April 29, 1996); Sarah C. Mavrinac and Neil R. Jones, with Marshall W. Meyer, "Competitive Renewal through Workplace Innovation: The Financial and Non-financial Returns to Innovative Workplace Practices," (Boston: Center for Business Innovation, Ernst & Young, LLP, June 1995); Jeff Mauzy, *Succeeding in Innovation: The Synectics Report on Creativity & Innovation in U. S. Corporations* (Cambridge, MA: The Synectics Corporation, 1993).

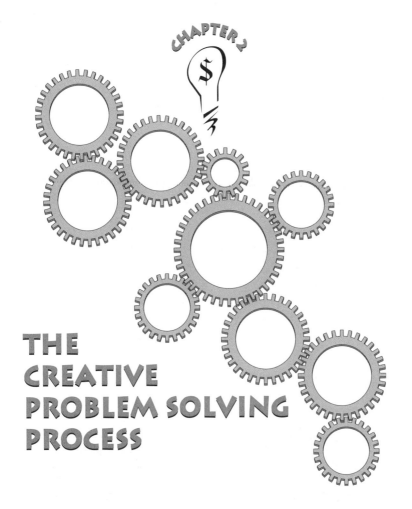

THE CREATIVE PROBLEM SOLVING PROCESS

Ultimately, innovation is about continually pushing back the boundaries of what is possible.

Michael J. Mandel
Business Week

Apple, 3M, Dell, IBM, Google, Nokia, P&G, Virgin, Samsung, Toyota, IDEO, and Starbucks are twelve of the most innovative firms in the world according to a survey of 940 senior executives in 68 countries conducted by the Boston Consulting Group.[1] The primary factor that separates these firms from the rest of the firms in the world is their ability to create and innovate successful products, services and processes over and over again.

They have mastered creative problem solving—the fundamental creativity skill. For individuals the development of creative problem-solving skills is a necessity not a luxury in the highly competitive employment environment of the 21ˢᵗ century. Because organizations too must solve problems in a highly competitive environment, the development of these skills in their members is also a necessity—organizations must become creative. The most creative and innovative individuals and organizations are the ones most likely to survive and prosper in the 21ˢᵗ century.

Problem solving is after all an integral part of organizational life. Every time a leader-manager directs people in producing a product or service, problems are being solved and decisions made. Every time any team or any individual member of an organization thinks of a new way to reduce costs, invents a new product or service, or determines how to help the organization function better in some way, problem solving is taking

Figure 2.1 The Creative Problem-Solving (CPS) Process

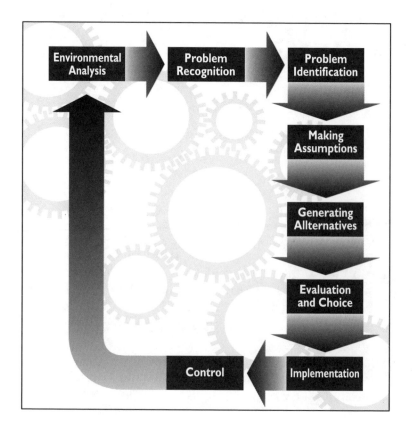

place. But whether the problem solving occurring in these situations is truly creative is another question. The answer is often "no" but that situation is changing as individuals and organizations have begun to integrate creativity and innovation into their daily regimens. This book provides creativity techniques that can assist both individuals and organizations in making problem solving a truly creative process. This chapter begins by describing the traditional problem-solving process as practiced by business people for many years. It then discusses how problem solving can be made more creative. It thus sets the stage for examining how problem solving can be made more creative through the use of creativity techniques.

CREATIVE PROBLEM SOLVING

Not too many years ago, problem solving was defined largely as a rational effort.[2] As scientists and management researchers tried to improve the problem-solving process, they focused on analysis and quantitative factors. But in recent years we have come to realize that a strictly rational approach misses the whole point of problem solving. Creativity is vital to successful problem solving. The problem-solving process therefore has come to be referred to more and more as the creative problem-solving process or CPS.

There are eight basic stages in the creative problem solving process: analyzing the environment, recognizing a problem, identifying the problem, making assumptions, generating alternatives, choosing among alternatives, implementing the chosen solution, and controlling for results. These stages are shown in Figure 2.1. The middle four of these stages are shown in the more detailed diagram presented in Figure 2.2. This figure provides more detail on these four stages primarily to show how the decision maker goes from problem identification and the selection of criteria to the actual choice of a decision. The following paragraphs briefly examine these stages from the practical viewpoint of problem solving within an organization. Personal, non-work-related problem solving would follow the same stages. Both analytical and creative processes are applicable to all eight stages.

Figure 2.2 Four Stages of the CPS Process

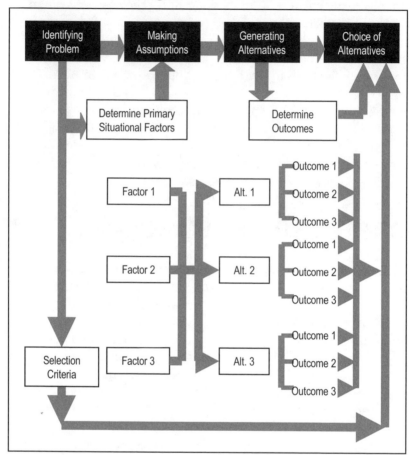

Analyzing the Environment

In this stage of the process, you are gathering information about what is going on in your organization and outside of it. If you are not constantly searching for problems and/or opportunities, how will you know that they exist? And how can you solve problems or take advantage of opportunities if you don't know they exist? We all know from personal experience that in the everyday world of business, we have to solve problems quickly; and we have to see the opportunities that are there and take advantage of them before somebody else does.

And at the corporate level, it's no different. Strategists know that firms must be flexible and must be prepared to respond quickly to problems and opportunities in order to be successful in the future, especially in turbulent environments.[3] And of course any changes made in strategy trickle down and become changes and hence creative problem solving situations for everyone else in the organization. Thus, it is absolutely vital to success that organizations and their employees be able to recognize problems and opportunities as soon as they occur, or better yet, even before they occur.

Just imagine yourself working for a company such as Finnish cell phone giant Nokia. It has been constantly bombarded by competitors seeking to take away its dominant market position. Managers and other employees at all levels of Nokia must be able to respond to this competition, but within an external environmental framework comprised of a myriad of other factors that are changing and must also be monitored, for example, the global economy, Finland's national economy, wage rates around the world, the availability of raw materials, and consumer tastes just to mention a few issues. The Creative Edge in Action 2.1 describes an effort by Nokia to analyze its environment and to formulate the appropriate strategy.

Nokia Seeks an Innovative Solution

One recent strategy chosen by Nokia was to target the top end of the market with a "smart phone," one that could perform more sophisticated functions than found in low end and medium level phones, for example, providing Internet connections and games that could be played on the cell phone. But their competitors focused on providing stylish models that included digital cameras that produced pictures with sharp images and yet were still priced for the middle segment of the market. Nokia's market share was clobbered by its competitors' strategies. Nokia's managers and other professionals had misgauged its environment. In some cases, Nokia's strategists simply didn't examine its external environment sufficiently and missed key points such as consumer tastes with respect to "smart phones." And in some cases Nokia simply disregarded or discounted environmental information. This happened when Nokia executives made the decision to stick with their unibody design rather than move to the increasingly popular clamshell design. Numerous subsequent decisions throughout the organization were made based on this faulty environmental analysis. Unfortunately for Nokia, many of these decisions led to failures in the market place.

But within months, Nokia countered with a new strategy that included a broader set of product offerings with the same kinds of features and cool designs that their competitors' cell phones had at lower prices. Still Nokia maintained their strategic focus on creating more functions for the high end cell phone believing that eventually consumers would demand them. They successfully relaunched their high end gaming phone providing more features and more exciting games. Such adjustments at the strategic level have led to numerous creative problem solving efforts at all levels of Nokia.

Sources: Editors, "Nokia Finally N-Gaged: Nokia Mobile Gaming Platform Finally Becomes Viable with a String of Hits," *Electronic Gaming Monthly*, (March 2005), p. 110; Nelson D. Schwartz, "Has Nokia Lost It?" *Fortune* (January 24, 2004), pp. 98-106; David Pringle, "Wrong Number: How Nokia Chased Top End of Market, Got Hit in Middle," *Wall Street Journal* (June 1, 2004), pp. A1, A10.

Recognizing a Problem or Opportunity

You need to be aware that a problem or opportunity exists before you can solve it or take advantage of it. It is from the information gathered in analyzing the environment that you will learn that a problem or opportunity exists. Often, however, the problem solver has only a vague feeling that something is wrong or that an opportunity exists. A gestation period seems to occur in which information from the environment is processed subconsciously and the existence of a problem or opportunity eventually registers at the conscious level.[4] For example, when Howard Schultz first bought Starbucks and turned it into a chain of pricey coffee shops, people thought he was crazy, but Schultz saw an opportunity. He wasn't sure there was one, but he intuited that there was. He was right. He turned Starbucks into a chain of 8500 stores with 90,000 employees with an increasing global presence. Now that everyone but Schultz thinks that he has saturated the market with his Starbucks coffee shops, Schultz see more opportunities for the firm with new products and new customers. Most would disagree, but he is focused on creating growth for the company through innovation.[5] Given his track record, his assumptions may just be right.

Identifying the Problem or Opportunity

The problem identification stage involves making sure the organization's efforts will be directed toward solving the real problem rather than merely eliminating symptoms.[6] This stage also involves establishing the objectives of the problem-solving process and determining what will constitute evidence that the problem has been solved. The outcome of this stage is a set of decision criteria for evaluating various options. See Figure 2.2.

Both rational and intuitive thinking may occur at this stage, but identification is largely a rational process. Key questions to be asked include the following:[7]

1.   What happened or will happen?
2.   Who does it or will it affect?
3.   Where did it or will it have an impact?
4.   When did it or will it happen?
5.   How did it or will it occur?
6.   Why did it or will it occur?
7.   What could we do to be more successful?

In asking these questions you are primarily interested in getting to the core problem or identifying the real opportunity. The benefits of doing so are aptly illustrated by the case of Hospital 'SWAT' teams discussed in the Creative Edge in Action 2.2.

CREATIVE EDGE IN ACTION 2.2

Hospital administrators at all levels of numerous hospitals suspected that a problem existed with respect to an increase in avoidable patient deaths, but the problem did not become clear or perhaps pressing until the analysis of statistics on a national level pointed to a serious and sizeable problem. Hospitals then recognized that a truly serious problem existed because thousands of patients were dying each year across the country from avoidable causes—both external and internal. Analysts believed that many if not most of these deaths could have been prevented if proper actions had been taken and/or mistakes had not been made. By thoroughly examining the avoidable death situations in their hospitals, administrators and staff found that the number of avoidable deaths that were occurring had increased for a number of reasons, including physician errors, incorrect drug prescriptions and/or errors in filling those prescriptions, overworked nursing staff, equipment failures, and for other reasons including hospital bureaucracy.

The number of critically ill patients who died was particularly troublesome since hospitals had for years focused so many resources on keeping these patients alive. Critically ill patients are those suffering from major illnesses or who have recently had surgery and are being constantly monitored in special care units or observed closely for signs of difficulty. What became evident once serious examination of hospital policies and procedures took place was that it was the system that was the problem, a system which had become bureaucratic in treating critically ill patients. For example, even though nurses and other staff saw signs of potential difficulty for the patient, they often called the attending physician and waited for his or her call back before taking actions to head off a major problem. Consequently, many times cardiac arrest would occur. Then highly skilled code teams would spring into action. It was generally believed that hospitals had become skilled at using code teams to save patients' lives once cardiac arrest occurred. But it became clear after further investigation that many of these patients were not saved by the code teams, and if they were, many eventually died in a few hours or a few days anyway.

Numerous hospitals around the country have now formed "SWAT" teams which cut through the bureaucracy to deliver significantly improved chances of recovery. These "rapid response teams are designed to prevent codes (cardiac arrest) and other medical crises from happening to begin with, by 'rescuing' patients at the first signs of a problem, rather than resuscitating them after the heart already has stopped." So now 'SWAT' teams comprised of nurses and other professional staff spring into action at the sign of "trigger" symptoms which are believed to lead to potential code or other crises without waiting for permission from a physician. By asking penetrating questions hospital administrators, doctors, nurses and professional staff have been able to identify the real problem behind the deaths of so many critically ill patients. In turn, they created a unique system for dealing with patient's crises.

Sources: Laura Landro, "Hospitals Form 'SWAT' Teams to Avert Deaths; Idea Is to Eliminate Red Tape That Slows Response to Problems; Lessons Learned From Australia" *Wall* Street Journal pp. D1, D5; Anonymous, "Report: Medical Mistakes Linked to 195,000 Deaths a Year," *Health Management Technology* (September, 2004) p. 10.

Making Assumptions

It is necessary to make assumptions about the condition of future factors in the problem situation. For example, what will the state of the economy be when the new product is to be launched? Or, how will your manager react to a suggestion? Remember that assumptions may be a major constraint on the potential success of a solution, or may cause you to overestimate the potential of a particular alternative to solve the problem effectively. As we saw with Nokia earlier in the chapter, assumptions are sometimes wrong but if properly revised, associated problems may be solved.

Swedish furniture maker Ikea, whose global customers assemble Ikea's furniture kits in order to save themselves money, has invested significant sums of money in Japan assuming it can entice Japan's 30-39 year old market (Ikea's primary market world-wide) into wanting to self-assemble furniture. Tommy Kullberg, CEO of Ikea Japan, shares the Ikea belief that the time is ripe for Ikea to become a major player in the Japanese furniture market despite the fact that the Japanese have historically not liked to assemble furniture, and that the Japanese have not historically been able to equate low prices with high quality. He claims, "That mentality has changed." Are Ikea's and Tommy Kullberg's assumptions correct? Only time and success will tell. But just in case it doesn't work, Ikea is offering an assembly service for the demanding Japanese consumer.[8]

Generating Alternatives

Generating alternatives involves cataloging the known options (a rational act) and generating additional options (a rational and intuitive act). *It is in this stage that most of the creativity techniques described in later chapters are extremely helpful.*

To the extent that you can clearly identify and formulate useful options, you can maximize the chances that a problem will be solved satisfactorily. The purpose of generating alternatives is to ensure that you reach the selection stage of CPS with enough potential solutions. Creativity techniques for generating alternatives can help you develop many more possible solutions than you might come up with otherwise.

Generating alternatives is partly a rational and partly an intuitive exercise. It's rational in that you follow a series of steps. It's intuitive in that these steps are designed to unleash your intuitive powers so that you can use them effectively.[9] In this stage, you should be more interested in the quantity of new ideas than in their quality. For most people, creativity reaches its highest levels in this stage of CPS. Creative Edge in Action 2.3 describes the process of service innovation at Bank of America and the ways that alternatives were generated and evaluated in their new banking services success story. What makes this such an interesting case study is that very few service companies actually do much R & D in the complete sense of those words. But Bank of America did, and did so successfully.

Choosing Among Alternatives

Decision making should be based on a systematic evaluation of the alternatives against the criteria established earlier. A key, very rational part of this process involves determining the possible outcomes of the various alternatives. (See Figure 2.2) This information is vital in making a decision. The better the job done

Bank of America—A Rare Look at Service Research and Development

With products, it is relatively easy to employ research and development methodologies in a laboratory. But it is very difficult to apply similar processes to services which are intangible, often exist only at the moment they are delivered, and are often customized for each customer making mass replication of the experiment difficult. To research and develop services as one would products requires turning an organization into a living laboratory, and that is exactly what Bank of America did in order to innovate new services. The bank formulated a five stage strategy for creating and innovating new services: conceive and evaluate ideas, plan and design the rollout of ideas for a local test market, implement these ideas, test these new services, and evaluate and roll them out to test markets nationwide.

Bank of America selected first 20, then an additional five branch banks from its Atlanta region to participate as living laboratories. Under the auspices of the bank's Innovation and Development team, a series of scientific experiments trying out new services on actual customers led to substantial customer satisfaction and growth opportunities for the bank. For example, using interviews and focus groups, the bank discovered that customer estimates of waiting times for services became exaggerated the longer the customer had to wait. Thus, a two minute wait seemed like a two minute wait to most customers, but a five minute wait seemed like a ten minute wait to a lot of customers. Using brainstorming and other creativity techniques, several ideas were generated and then evaluated. One suggestion was to "entertain" customers while they were in line. It was hypothesized that customers, having been entertained, would lower their estimates of waiting times. Customers were entertained in some of the subject banks, and the hypothesis turned out to be true. The conclusion of this experiment was that customer dissatisfaction levels could be lowered by "entertaining" them while they waited for services.

As with any scientific experiment, control factors and decision criteria had to be utilized. For example, "noise" going on around the experiment had to be filtered out during the results analysis process, and the costs of implementation had to be considered. All in all, about one half of the new services tested were deemed appropriate for national test market roll-out.

Source: Stefan Thomke, "R&D Comes to Services: Bank of America's Pathbreaking Experiments," *Harvard Business Review* (April 2003), pp. 71-79.

CREATIVE EDGE IN ACTION 2.3

in generating alternatives and determining their possible outcomes, the greater is the chance that an effective choice will be made. The choice process is mostly rational, but very skilled decision makers rely on intuition as well, especially for complex problems. Such was the case at Bank of America as discussed in Creative Edge in Action 2.3.

Implementing Solutions

Once you have a clear idea of what you want to do and a plan for accomplishing it, you can take action. Implementation requires persistent attention. This means accounting for details and anticipating and overcoming obstacles. Set specific goals and reasonable deadlines, and gain the support of others for your solution. Implementation is a series of problems and opportunities. The processes described in this book are applicable to each of these.

When Darden Restaurants began a new leadership initiative aimed at changing the leadership styles of its managers, it commenced this initiative with a trial leadership development program for its Olive Garden chain. This program was provided by the Crummer Graduate School of Business at Rollins College. Finding the program to be not only satisfactory but even inspiring, it then rolled out this program for all managers in the Olive Garden chain. Eventually managers in all of its restaurant chains will go through the program.[10]

Controlling for Results

Evaluating results is the final, and an often overlooked stage in the creative problem-solving process. The purpose of the evaluation is to determine the extent to which the actions you took have solved the problem. This stage feeds directly into the problem-finding stage, which begins a new cycle of creative problem solving. It is important at this stage to be able to recognize deficiencies in your own solutions if necessary. If you can admit to making mistakes or changing your mind without feeling defensive or embarrassed, you have acquired the skill of open minded adaptation. This often requires objective thinking, intellectual courage, and self-confidence. At Federal Express, group decisions based on CPS are part of the everyday routine, and so is control. For example when one team solved problems related to sorting packages, they were required to track results and make further improvements.[11]

TWO KINDS OF THINKING

Within all of the eight stages of the CPS process, there are two distinct kinds of thought processes: divergent and convergent as shown in Figure 2.3.[12] Divergent thinking means expanding the picture of the problem. It is essentially a right-brain activity and involves stating the problem in various forms, looking at it from various points of view, gathering information, and generating numerous options for solving it. For example, think of the orange.

Now think of twenty disparate uses for this fruit that don't include eating it. This is divergent thinking. Divergent thinking leads to more and broader perspectives. Convergent thinking means narrowing down the problem and related parts of its solution, to a more manageable size and perspective. It is essentially a left-brain activity and involves evaluating options. For example, if you now determine which of your twenty uses for the orange is "best," then you would be engaging in convergent thinking. Convergent thinking is reductive because it creates smaller and more detailed pictures from which to prepare for action. Too much convergent thinking and you are trapped with a limited number of quality alternatives.

Both types of thinking are important to effective creative problem solving. One of the most important skills in problem solving is knowing when to use each. If you can combine divergent and convergent modes of thinking and use them flexibly according to the situation, you will be progressing toward mental integration—combining the skills of an innovator with the skills of the practical realist. Both divergent and convergent modes of thinking utilize both conscious and subconscious thought processes.

In our schools and organizations we mostly teach convergent thinking. We are, as a society, weak in divergent thinking. This book is about increasing your divergent thinking. Creativity techniques are for the most part divergent thinking techniques. Several exist for all eight stages of creative problem solving.

INCORPORATING CREATIVITY INTO PROBLEM SOLVING

Experience with problem solving has produced some discouraging findings. Among them are the following:

1. Creativity is not a major part of the problem-solving process for most organizations or individuals.
2. People are not usually encouraged to be creative, either as individuals or as members of organizations. This means that creativity is discouraged in most organizations including families, schools and companies.
3. Few people really know the creativity techniques that can be applied in the problem-solving process.
4. Few individuals develop their personal creative problem-solving skills, but that is changing.
5. Few organizations train their employees in creative problem solving or in creativity techniques.

It is evident that most people, as well as most organizations, can improve their CPS skills significantly. Fortunately an increasing number of individuals and organizations now recognize the criticality of creativity as the source of innovation and innovation as the source of competitiveness and growth. We are witnessing an evolution wherein organizations are moving more and more toward a focus on design and a focus on

Figure 2.3 Divergence and Convergence

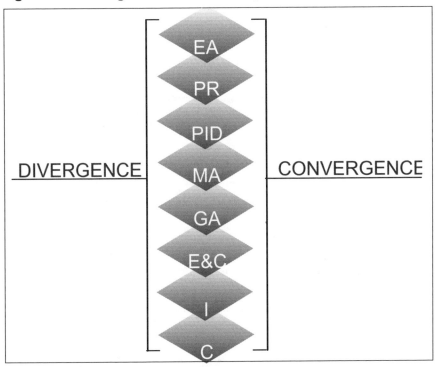

the ability to continuously innovate new products and services. To do both of these requires creativity. [13]

As mentioned in Chapter 1, individuals can go through a series of 9 steps to become more creative, for example, accepting their innate creativity, unlearning how not to be creative, and so on. These 9 steps assist the problem-solver, opportunity-finder in going through the eight stage creative problem-solving process. The fourth of the 9 steps is the subject of this book—creativity techniques. These offer the most immediate impact of any of the nine steps. Note that these creativity techniques help with all eight stages of the creative problem-solving process, enabling numerous new ways of accomplishing each of those eight stages.

Groups and teams can also go through a series of steps to become better at group problem solving.[14] But for quick improvement in their levels of creativity, groups and teams should employ the creativity techniques discussed in this book as they go through the CPS process.

Organizations that want to become more creative have a much more difficult task than individuals and groups seeking to achieve the same objective. For most organizations becoming creative requires a major overall of the organization's context, but especially its culture, leadership style, and performance man-agement systems. Creativity needs to become part of the culture, leader-managers need to seek it and reward it in their employees, and the organization must seek it and re-ward it through its performance management systems. The organization's values must incorporate creativity and innova-tion, and its cultural artifacts, for example, the stories told about what leads to success in the organization and the reward sys-tems of the organization, must be changed to incorporate cre-ativity and innovation.

IDEO is a product/service development firm that has created a large number of successful new products and services for a wide range of companies. Among some of its better known products and services are: the first mouse for Apple Macintosh, the Humulin Insulin Pen, the Palm V product design, interac-tive dressing rooms for haute couturier Prada, the stand-up tooth paste tube for Procter & Gambel's Crest brand, Steelcase's "leap chair," Oral B Toothbrushes for kids, and the redesign of emergency rooms for healthcare giant Kaiser Permanente. Because of its success with so many product designs and re-designs, IDEO has not become a model for creative problem solving in the organization. They offer seminars, workshops, and consultancies to develop their process for other organiza-tions. Creative Edge in Action 2.4 highlights the key points of the IDEO creativity process.

Organizations that choose to use the IDEO process almost al-ways need to change their organization's context for innova-tion, but especially culture, leadership style and performance management systems. And they must have a staff which is willing and able to provide the intensity, energy, diversity, ex-perience and competence that the IDEO staff possesses.

IDEO's Creativity Process

The IDEO creativity process mirrors the eight stage CPS process to a great extent. Their process is a high-energy group process based on these five steps:

1. Observation: extensive information gathering and analysis of customer needs, wants, and actions. Behavioral science is critical in this stage. IDEO team members: shadow consumers as they use related products, video people as they engage in the consumer process, ask consumers to keep video diaries of their consumption activities, have consumers tell stories about their consumer experiences, use diverse groups of consumers to build an experience base.

2. Brainstorming: intense, usually one-hour sessions based on the rules of basic brainstorming (see Chapter 5), but incorporating many of the elements of other techniques described in this book. The basic rules of brainstorming are strictly enforced. In addition, they try to use lots of color when writing up their ideas; they stay focused on the subject; and only one conversation can go on at a time—interruptions are not allowed.

3. Rapid Prototyping: mockups of solutions are created; often videos are used to demonstrate services or new products. They build mock-ups quickly and cheaply. There are no frills on the prototypes. They create scenarios to show how consumers might use a service. They role play various consumer types using products and services.

4. Refining: brainstorming is used to narrow the number of solutions. Solutions may be combined. Customers are involved in this stage. This all takes place quickly. They are disciplined and ruthless in narrowing the field. They focus on outcomes and get agreement from all stakeholders.

5. Implementation: an actual product or service is created bringing all of the diverse talent of the team's members to bear on the problem or opportunity. One key here is that the workforce is extremely diverse in backgrounds enabling creative implementation ideas to evolve quickly.

Beyond understanding the basics of this process, it is vital to understand the energy, intensity, experience and competency brought to the situation by IDEO staff. They make it happen.

CREATIVE EDGE IN ACTION 2.4

CONTINUED ON PAGE 38

While it is relatively easy to see how this process could be used with products, it is also readily applicable to services. IDEO has expanded into services in recent years. The keys have been to observe and study the interaction of the customer in the existing situation (step 1), and then use the other four steps to bring creativity to the solutions of service development problems. IDEO has worked with a wide range of companies from Warnaco (redesign of the lingerie department in stores that feature Warnaco products) to hospitals (redesign of emergency room process and design for healthcare giant Kaiser Permanente facilities).

As client companies witnessed the success of this process as IDEO developed new products and services for them, they began asking IDEO to teach them this process. Others heard of the IDEO process, and now IDEO is beginning to have a major impact on numerous corporate cultures throughout the U.S. and increasingly in Europe and Asia as well.

Source: Bruce Nussbaum, "The Power of Design," *Business Week* (May 17, 2004), pp. 86-93

101 CPS TECHNIQUES

Creativity techniques can be applied in all stages of the CPS process: analyzing the environment, recognizing the problem, making assumptions, generating alternatives, choosing among alternatives, implementing the chosen solution, and control. Many techniques exist for generating alternative solutions, while only a few wxist for each of these other stages. This book reflects these levels of availability focusing mostly on techniques for generating alternatives but providing some techniques for each of the other stages. The remaining chapters of this book will describe **101** creativity techniques that, when used at the appropriate stage of CPS, can greatly improve the results of that process.   **70** of the **101** techniques described are used to generate alternatives.

Chapter 3 describes techniques for the first 3 stages of the CPS model: analyzing the environment, recognizing that a problem exists, and identifying the problem. Chapters 4 and 5 discuss techniques for generating creative alternatives.

Chapter 4 focuses on individual techniques, Chapter 5 on group techniques which have been shown to be useful in raising levels of creativity. Most techniques can be used by individuals or groups, and that these designations merely reflect the most common usage of these techniques. Chapter 6 reviews creative approaches to choice, implementation and control. Chapter 7 discusses some of the practical aspects of using these techniques.

The lengthier discussions in all of these chapters focus on the best-known, more difficult to understand, or most often used techniques. For longer and/or more complicated techniques a summary of the steps necessary appears at the end of the discussion of that technique. In this and other chapters, techniques are presented in alphabetical order within sections to make them easier to find. Remember that techniques are numbered twice. The first number denotes the technique's position from 1 to 101, the second number is the technique's position within that stage of the problem solving model.

REFERENCES

[1] Bruce Nussbaum, "Get Creative," *Business Week* (August 1, 2005), pp. 63-64.

[2] This discussion is based on several sources. For an extensive review see Joseph A.Tainter, "Problem Solving: Complexity, History, Sustainability," *Population and Environment* (September 2000), pp. 3-33. Also see E. Frank (New York: McGraw-Hill, 1962); Charles Kepner and Benjamin Tregoe, *The Rational Manager* (New York: McGraw-Hill, 1965).

[3] Rosemary T. Skordoulis, "Strategic Flexibility and Change: An Aid to Strategic Thinking or Another Managerial Abstraction, "*Strategic Change* (August 2004), pp. 253-258; Michael Nastanski, "The Value of Active Scanning to Senior Executives: Insights from Key Decision-Makers," *The Journal of Management Development* (Bradford: 2004, Issue 5/6), p. 426 contains a representative discussion; Andrew Bolger, "Failure to Look Ahead Increases Risk to Business", *Financial Times* (June 2, 2004), "FT Risk Management," p. 1; *Torben Juul Andersen*, "Integrating the Strategy Formation Process: An International Perspective," *European Management Journal* (London: June 2004), pp. 263-26; Brent Dreyer, "Uncertainty, Flexibility, and Sustained Competitive Advantage, *Journal of Business Research* (May 2004), pp. 484-495.

[4] David A. Cowan, "Developing a Process Model of Problem Recognition," *Academy of Management Review* (October 1986), pp. 763-776.

[5] Abrahm Lustgarten, Brian Dumaine, Julie Creswell, Christopher Tkaczyk, et. al., "14 Innovators," *Fortune* (November 15, 2004), pp. 192-197; Steven Gray,

"Starbucks Posts 49% Rise in Net on Innovations," *Wall Street Journal* (November 11, 2004). p. B.5; Andy Serwer, "Hot Starbucks to Go," *Fortune* (January 26, 2004), pp. 60-74.

[6] Charles Kepner and Benjamin Tregoe, *The New Rational Manager* (New York: McGraw-Hill, 1989); Cowan, op. cit.

[7] Ibid. for the first six items. The seventh is aimed at opportunity recognition and identification.

[8] Mariko Sanchanta, "Ikea's Second Try at Japan's Flat-Pack Fans," *Financial Times* (March 4, 2004), p. 11.

[9] Eugene Sadler-Smith and Erella Shefy, "The Intuitive Executive: Understanding and Applying 'Gut Feel' in Decision-making," *Academy of Management Executive* (November 2004), pp. 76-91.

[10] My discussion with the head of executive development at the Crummer School, April 2005. .

[11] Martha T. Moore, "Sorting Out a Mess," *USA Today* (April 10, 1992), p. 5B.

[12] For an in-depth discussion see Gordon S. Bonner, *Implementing Innovative Solutions: Harvesting Acres of Diamonds* (Buffalo, New York: Creative Education Foundation, 1990), pp. 2-31

[13] Bruce Nussbaum, "Get Creative: How to Build Innovative Companies," *Business Week* (August 1, 2005), pp. 60-85.

[14] For example see: Jill Nemiro, *Creativity in Virtual Teams : Key Components for Success* (San Francisco: Pfeiffer: 2004); Barbara J. Streibel, Brian L. Joiner, Peter R. Scholtes, *The Team Handbook* (Madison, WI: Joiner/Oriel, Inc. 2003); John Whatmore, *Releasing Creativity: How Leaders Can Develop Creative Potential in Their Teams* (London: Kogan-Page, 1999); Eric Skopec and Dayle M. Smith, *How to Use Team Building to Foster Innovation Throughout Your Organization* (Chicago: Contemporary Books, 1997); and Gregory P. Smith, *The New Leader: Bring Creativity and Innovation to the Workplace* (Delray Beach, FL: St. Lucie Press, 1997).

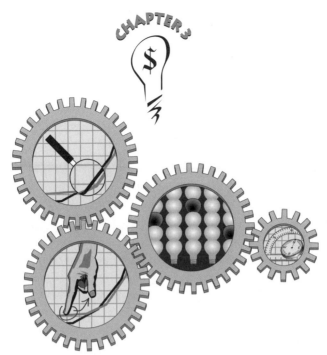

CREATIVE TECHNIQUES
FOR
ANALYZING THE ENVIRONMENT, RECOGNIZING & IDENTIFYING PROBLEMS, AND MAKING ASSUMPTIONS

Research shows creativity can be taught and companies are listening. - *Emily T. Smith,et.al., Business Week*

It is very easy for an organization to fail when it is extremely successful. Business history is replete with stories of firms that have followed this path. At one time General Motors "owned" the U.S. auto market with a 60% market share. More recently its share has hovered around 24%. GM failed to fully analyze and fully comprehend what Japanese automobile firms could do to its market dominance. At one time, Digital Equipment Corporation (DEC) dominated the mini-computer segment of the computer industry; now DEC is but a memory. DEC's top management dismissed the PC as irrelevant, believing it posed no threat. But as PC speed and memory improved, the need for the mini-computer diminished. DEC not only failed to recognize a problem, but also an opportunity. Ironically a failing DEC was acquired by Compaq, a PC company, not for its hardware division but for its service division which Compaq saw as important in the PC business. Compaq later became part of HP/Compaq.

None of the major airlines faced up to the innovation that Southwest brought to the airline industry when they should have. Now, for many it is too late. And Sony, as successful as it has been, is losing market share in many product markets and it seems to have lost its ability to be first to market with innovative new products. These firms and a multitude of others failed to either perform an adequate environmental analysis, recognize that a problem existed, identify the underlying problem, and/or make appropriate assumptions about the situation.

You cannot solve a problem or take advantage of an opportunity until you know it exists and that you are solving the underlying, causal problem. You cannot be creative in generating alternatives until you have a reason to do so. You will not be successful unless you make the right assumptions.

TECHNIQUES FOR ANALYZING THE ENVIRONMENT

The creativity techniques discussed in this chapter are to be used to creatively analyze the environment, recognize that a problem or opportunity exists, identify the core problem or opportunity, and to make assumptions. The rational techniques for environmental analysis focus on control processes and environmental scanning. In recent years, the use of computers to gather and analyze data has become an integral part of this approach. Enterprise Resource Accounting systems, such as those sold by SAP, focus on internal information. Various competitor intelligence software pro-grams focus on that part of the external environment. Benchmarking and best practices, which were featured as creative ways of comparing ones company against others in the first edition of this book, have become quite common business practices in recent years. In benchmarking a firm compares its practices with those of the firm that is considered the best in its industry. In best practices, a firm compares itself with the firm that is considered the best at certain practices, regardless of the industry in which it operates. The results of these comparisons are used to guide and motivate change and as target objectives for improvement.[1] Several websites are devoted to best practices, for example, see: bestpractices@best-in-class.com. Some of these websites offer research information about best practices in selected industries.

The following are more creative approaches to environmental analysis than most with which you will be familiar.

1/1. COMPARISON AGAINST OTHERS: LISTENING TO EMPLOYEES AND CUSTOMERS; RACING AGAINST PHANTOM COMPETITORS

Listening to employees to find out what is happening in the marketplace is something that a number of companies have done for years, but the employees listened to are typically sales force members. Nokia has expanded this technique in a creative way. Simon Beresford-Wylie, senior vice-president for Nokia Asia-Pacific, indicates that Nokia routinely listens to all of its 50,000 employees regardless of their position in the company to find out what they have observed in the marketplace. This information is then used by its R&D

FIRM A.

group to fashion new designs and products.[2] This knowledge helps the firm position itself against its competitors.

Many companies now work with customers to find out what they need in order to enhance product development efforts. But some companies now also work with customers to discover what their competitors are up to, to find out what is being offered these customers in the marketplace. Largely ignored until recently, Customer Relationship Management (CRM) should not only involve listening to customer needs, but should also involve listening to find out what the competition is doing. This knowledge also helps the firm position itself against its competitors.

Finally, when he was head of the Bonneville Power Administration, Peter T. Johnson created a fictitious super competitor with which to compare his organization.[3] Other firms create a composite super competitor taking the best practices in different areas and combining them. These are unique ways of engaging in best practices.

2/2. HIRE FUTURISTS AND OTHER CONSULTANTS

No one says you have to discover problems or opportunities yourself. Why not hire someone to perform this task for you? There are numerous futurists and other consultants who can guide you. They often bring a fresh perspective. For example, they may be able to see the forest for the trees, something someone close to the situation may not be able to do.

3/3. MONITOR WEAK SIGNALS

A standard strategic planning technique is to pay careful attention to weak signals in the market. Forecasters, clipping services, customers, employees, networks and computer searches can keep you informed. Attending seminars can perform a similar function. And software programs exist to analyze all sorts of data that predicts future events. For example, there exist a number of software programs to predict new technologies that may be coming into existence. Firms use these to assist their own product development programs.[4] Many real estate developers are in 2006 questioning what appear to be weak signals of a housing market bubble about to burst. Recognizing and identifying problems and opportunities are two different skills. Acting on these requires another set of skills.

4/4. OPPORTUNITY SEARCHES

Active opportunity searches can turn up new situations and new applications of current knowledge. You don't have to be limited to traditional sources. Try something new, like the manager who searches science fiction literature to find ideas that are applicable to his high-tech business. Try simply reading about new trends and asking what this means to your business. For example, what opportunities are created for your company by global warming?

TECHNIQUES FOR
RECOGNIZING PROBLEMS

Many people recognize that a problem exists when they have failed to meet an objective or believe they may fail to meet an objective. The purpose of most control reports is to provide such comparisons. People may recognize an opportunity when they become aware that they could exceed their objectives by choosing a certain alternative or taking advantage of a situation.

Frequently individuals compare current performance with prior objectives, prior experience, or last year's performance in order to determine whether a problem exists. When they see a difference between the current situation and what was previously thought appropriate, they recognize that a problem exists.[5] IBM for example, has recently released a series of new software products aimed at helping companies recognize and identify business problems.[6]

Fully describing current conditions is another way of being able to recognize a problem or opportunity. Simply reviewing the existing situation may provide some insight into problems or potential problems. This seems obvious, but few people actually do it.

The following paragraphs describe more creative techniques for recognizing problems. Some are traditional approaches; others are new twists on approaches you may already be familiar with. Several involve ways of analyzing the environment in search of opportunities.

5/1.   CAMELOT

Create an idealized situation, a Camelot. Now compare it to the existing situation. What are the differences? Why do they exist? What problems or opportunities are suggested by the differences?[7]

6/2.   CHECKLISTS

Using a checklist when examining a situation can be extremely beneficial. A number of checklists have been developed for this purpose. For example, in their book, *That's a Great Idea,* Tony Husch and Linda Foust provide numerous checklists designed to improve situation analysis. Among other things, their checklists provide guidance in finding opportunities, recognizing certain problems, generating new-product ideas, generating promotional ideas, and evaluating ideas.[8] Other checklists include strategic audits which examine strategy, management audits which examine overall management actions, quality audits which examine quality compliance, and social audits which examine for socially responsible activities.[9] Finally, Arthur B. VanGundy has provided a Product Improvement Checklist.[10] By using the checklist to compare what could be done to a product to what currently exists, a manager can identify problems and opportunities. VanGundy's list can also be used to generate creative alternatives and is discussed in more detail in Chapter 4.

Does creative recognition of a problem help in solving it? Of course it does, as Creative Edge in Action 3.1 suggests.

Reviewing Reports for Weak Signals

Part of being able to recognize that a problem exists is learned intuition-a kind of subconscious screening and melding of experiences. Managers with that type of intuition might recognize that a problem existed after examining information that others would not even give a second thought to.

Lou Gerstner, at that time CEO of IBM, was at home on a Sunday afternoon in 1999 reading monthly reports from the various divisions. Buried deep in one of the reports, he found one line saying that pressures to meet current objectives had caused the unit to cut costs by ceasing its efforts on a promising new product area. Gerstner became incensed. He wanted to know how often that was happening. J. Bruce Harreld, as head of strategy for IBM, was charged with finding out the answer to that question. Quite often was the answer that Harreld uncovered; way too often to suit Gerstner. IBM was known as a company that was great at R&D and securing patents but not very strong in delivering products.

Gerstner decided to change all of that. He wanted to know what the root causes were and how to fix them. Harreld soon found out that IBM's bottom-line focused culture was partly to blame-there was tremendous pressure to make the numbers. Also he discovered that the company was putting its best managers at the head of mature businesses and putting less experienced managers at the top of new, potential high-growth companies. All of that experience was being wasted on easier to run businesses. Time consuming actions were taken to correct these and related problems and situations. Samuel J. Palmisano who followed Gerstner as CEO, accelerated the process. The results have been nothing short of spectacular. By 2005, IBM had launched 25 "emerging business opportunities" or EBO's. 22 of them were successful and were producing annual revenues of $15 billion with an average 40% per year growth rate. Is creative problem recognition and identification vital? Absolutely.

Source: Alan Deutschman, "Building a Better Skunk Works," *Fast Company* (March 2005), pp. 68-74.

CREATIVE EDGE IN ACTION 3.1

7/3. INVERSE BRAINSTORMING

Read the section on brainstorming at the beginning of Chapter 5. Inverse brainstorming is a variant of the approach described there. Whereas regular brainstorming begins with a problem and looks for a solution, inverse brainstorming begins with a situation and looks for potential problems, such as lack of motivation in the work force.[11] In other words, you take what appears to be a satisfactory situation and see what you can find wrong with it.

8/4. LIMERICKS AND PARODIES

Make up limericks and parodies about a situation. People can't resist poking fun, and when they do so, problems may be revealed. For example, one employee used the theme song from "The Music Man" to poke fun at managers in his organization. He rewrote the song along these lines: "Trouble. We've got trouble right here in River City. It starts with an 'm' and ends with a 't,' it's management. Yes sir, trouble right here in River City." He secretly distributed copies of his song to his fellow employees and to top management. An investigation followed, and two especially bad managers were replaced.

9/5. LISTING COMPLAINTS

One effective way of uncovering problems is to have employees, customers, or other constituents brainstorm a list of complaints, either individually or in groups. (See Chapter 5 for a description of brainstorming.) Another version of this approach is to have employees list stumbling blocks that they have encountered.[12]

10/6. RESPONDING TO SOMEONE ELSE

Sometimes people bring you problems or opportunities that deserve careful consideration even if they seem farfetched. In some businesses this happens quite often. Stories abound of cases in which people have failed to recognize the potential of ideas brought to them by others. As noted earlier, George Lucas took the "Star Wars" idea to twelve movie studios before Fox decided to produce it. IBM, General Motors, and DuPont were all offered the xerography idea and rejected it as impossible and unnecessary. So Chester Carlson and his associates went into business for themselves and became multimillionaires. Victor Kiam was offered a chance to buy the patent to Velcro for $25,000 but failed to see its potential. 13 Velcro applications are now estimated at hundreds of millions of dollars per year.[13]

The moral of these stores: Listen to others. Envision the possibilities.

11/7. ROLE PLAYING

Role playing requires you to pretend you are someone else. You may role play with another person in an interactive learning situation much like a play, or by simply imagining another person's situation and walking through it in your mind. Putting yourself in someone else's shoes-for example, a customer's-may give you totally new insights into a situation. It may allow you to solve potential problems before they become real ones. Imagine that you are someone else in the problem situation. Describe the problem from that person's perspective. Now solve it from that perspective. What new insights did you gain?

12/8. SUGGESTION PROGRAMS

From the standpoint of the organization, the suggestion program offers a tremendous opportunity to learn about the existence of problems and to obtain some solutions. But such programs must be implemented effectively. Japanese firms have really good suggestion programs. Some U.S. firms, such as Lockheed, also have good programs. Today's suggestion programs are themselves creative and offer the organization many opportunities to solve problems, save money, and innovate new products and services.[14]

13/9. WORKOUTS AND OTHER GROUP APPROACHES

GE has developed a process known as the workout. Workouts involve a three-day retreat in which managers and their subordinates gather to solve problems experienced by the work unit. It is a highly participative effort with a unique twist. Subordinates suggest the causes of the problems and recommend solutions. On the third day these are presented to their manager, whose superior manager is also in attendance sitting behind his or her subordinate but facing the employees. The workout manager must choose among three responses to subordinates' recommendations: Yes, no, or let's examine it and make a decision by a specific date. Deferrals are discouraged.[15] The workout manager must make a decision about employee suggestions without knowing what his or her boss's reactions are because of how the two managers are seated. Other group techniques (such as creativity circles, described in Chapter 5) can also be used to recognize problems. Simple group discussion may lead to both recognition and identification.

TECHNIQUES FOR IDENTIFYING PROBLEMS

Identifying the problem means making certain that your actions will be directed toward solving the real problem or taking advantage of the real opportunity, rather than merely addressing symptoms of the problem or an apparent (but not necessarily real) opportunity. Problem identification requires careful analysis.

A well-known set of identification techniques has been sug-gested by Charles Kepner and Benjamin Tregoe, who believe that correctly identifying the problem is the most important step in creative problem solving. Their approach, described in their book, *The Rational Manager*, begins by asking what's different now than before; this is followed by what, where, when, how, and why questions. Kepner and Tregoe like to use the example of a ball bearing manufacturing facility that began finding impurities in some of its ball bearings. The company replaced the machine that manufac-tured the ball bearings, but impurities continued to appear. Eventually, after answering the "when" question, the company's manag-ers determined that the impurities occurred only at periodic intervals. After asking and answering the other questions, they discovered that an air-freshening unit was blowing impurities into the molten metal; the unit came on only at certain times during the day.[16]

This section describes twelve techniques that can be used in the problem identification stage of creative problem solv-ing.

14/1. BOUNCE IT OFF SOMEONE ELSE

Simply talking to someone else about a problem employs the idea that "two heads are better than one." Suggest what you think the problem is and elicit the other person's reac-tion. Each of you can offer definitions and defend them un-til you find one that you can agree on.

15/2. CONSENSUS BUILDING

A large number of techniques for consensus building exist. Among these are: voting in a democratic manner and sitting in a circle and discussing the problem until a consensus is reached.

16/3. DRAW PICTURE OF THE PROBLEM

One way to make certain that you are identifying the real problem is to draw a picture of it. This process can also be used in generating alternatives. Because creativity is largely a right-brain function (in right-handed people, sometimes the opposite in left-handed people), and the right brain is more visually oriented than the left brain, (again often opposite for left-handers) drawing pictures seems to aid the creative process. If you can "see" the problem, you have a better chance of making certain that you are solving the real problem. So take out a pen and a piece of paper and draw a picture of your problem. What insights do you gain?

17/4. EXPERIENCE KIT

The experience kit was developed by IdeaScope of Cambridge, Massachusetts. It involves putting problem solvers through an experience that causes them to understand the problem better and therefore generate more and better solutions. It is a sort of combination of role playing and idea triggers. The experience kit involves participants in the problem. For example, IdeaScope provided detergent brand managers trying to improve their products' sales with an experience kit consisting of a sample of competitors' products; a diary for recording when the participants' own households did laundry in a week and how big the loads were; the requirement to visit a local laundry company (address provided) for at least one hour; and a dirty shirt that had to be washed at home using the company's product and then worn to the creativity session. Several of the spots on the shirts wouldn't come out. All of the experiences provided the brand managers with new insights into the problem.[17]

18/5. FISHBONE DIAGRAM

Two very useful approaches to identifying problems are the fishbone diagram and the related why-why diagram. (The latter will be discussed near the end of this chapter.) The fishbone diagram, sometimes referred to as the Ishikawa diagram, was developed by Professor Kaoru Ishikawa of the University of Tokyo.[18] The primary purpose of this exercise is to identify and list all the possible causes of the problem at hand. This is primarily a group problem identification technique, but it can be used by individuals as well.

This process is called the fishbone diagram because of the unique way in which the information gathered is arranged visually. When the problem and its causes are recorded, they form a diagram that resembles the skeleton of a fish. The problem is written down and enclosed in a circle on the right side of a sheet of paper. A straight line is drawn to the left and appears much like the backbone of a fish. (See Figure 3.1 for an abbreviated example of a fishbone diagram.) The next step involves drawing stems at a 45 degree angle to the backbone line. At the end of each of these stems are listed all of the causes of the problem that can be brainstormed. Additional stems may be added if necessary. Branches can be placed on each stem for further breakdowns of each cause. The causes should be listed with the least complicated nearest the head of the fish and the most complicated at the tail, with those in between listed on a continuum from least to most complicated.

The fishbone diagram can be brainstormed over more than one session. Ishikawa describes the process as one in which "you write your problem down on the head of the fish and then let it cook overnight." If the technique is employed over two or more sessions, new ideas may arise from three main effects: (1) There is time for the subconscious to work on the problem; (2) participants are likely to be less inhibited as the authorship of particular contributions will be forgotten; and (3) people may become more immersed in the problem if they think about it day and night.

When the diagram is completed, the individual or group begins to analyze the stems and the branches to determine the real problem or problems that need to be solved. If simpler problems are examined first, they can be removed from consideration before more complicated problems are tackled. If the problem solver(s) decide that certain causes are more significant than others, these will be given more attention in the alternative generation stage of CPS.

The fishbone diagram is extremely useful for identifying problems for several reasons:

1. It encourages problem solvers to study all parts of a problem before making a decision.

2. It helps show the relationships between causes and the relative importance of those causes.

3. It helps start the creative process because it focuses the problem solver(s) on the problem.

4. It helps start a logical sequence for solving a problem.

5. It helps problem solvers see the total problem as opposed to focusing on a narrow part of it.

6. It offers a way to reduce the scope of the problem and solve less complex issues rather than more complex ones.

7. It helps keep people focused on the real problem rather than going off on tangents.

When you first use the fishbone diagram, begin with small, readily definable problems and move to more complex issues as you learn the process.

Figure 3.1 FishBone Diagram

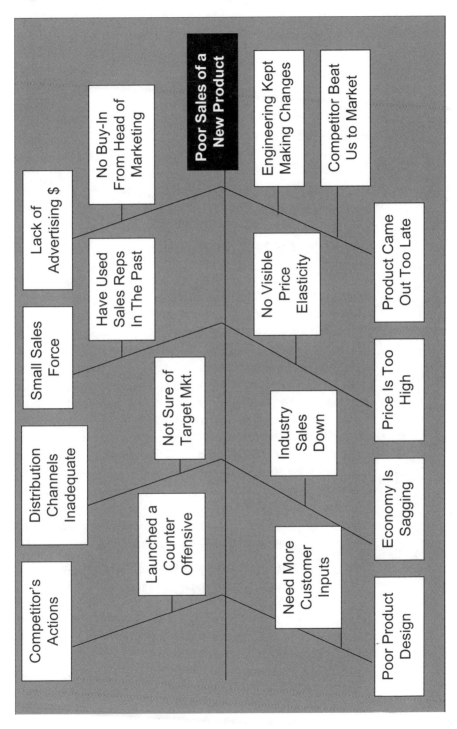

19/6. KING OF THE MOUNTAIN

King of the mountain is a children's game in which one player gets on top of something, such as a stump or a chair, and the others try to knock him or her off. A similar game can be used as a problem identification technique.[19] One or two individuals take a position on what the problem is, and other members of the group attempt to knock them off their definitional "mountain." To succeed in doing so, the challenger must have a better definition of the problem. Just as in the game, once someone has knocked another person off the mountain, he or she must get on top of the mountain. His or her ideas are then attacked until another challenger succeeds in becoming "king of the mountain." The survivor, who might have modified any of the ideas presented earlier, possesses what is now a group consensus regarding the true nature of the problem.

20/7. REDEFINING A PROBLEM OR OPPORTUNITY

Redefine a problem in as many ways as you possibly can. Perhaps this will help you see it in another light. Imagine it from the perspective of someone who is less familiar with it. Say the new definition aloud. Perhaps you'll hear something in what you're saying that you haven't noticed before. Try to determine how you feel about it. Pretend that you don't know what the problem is but do know some of the variables involved. If you were a member of another profession, how would you view the problem? How many different ways can you express this problem or opportunity? Now go back and examine what you have done. Do you see the problem any differently?

The following exercise can get you started in applying this technique. Think of a problem or opportunity and restate it five different ways:

1. _____

2. _____

3. _____

4. _____

5. _____

21/8. REWRITE OBJECTIVES IN DIFFERENT WAYS

In order to make certain that you are really addressing the underlying problem, you can rewrite your objectives or other criteria in several different ways. For example, if your problem is to increase productivity, this might be restated as: increase sales per employee, cut costs, how do I increase productivity, be more efficient, be more effective, set better goals, and so on.

22/9. SQUEEZE AND STRETCH

As part of the problem-solving process, you can try "squeezing" and "stretching" the problem.[20] Thinking in terms of squeezing and stretching allows you to analyze a problem better. You squeeze a problem to find its basic components. You stretch the problem in order to discover more of its scope.

CHAPTER

3

To squeeze a problem, ask a chain of questions beginning with the word "why."

Example:

Question:	*Why am I doing this?*
Answer:	Because I want to.
Question:	*Why do I want to.*
Answer:	Because I have been told to by my boss.
Question:	*Why does my boss want me to do it?*
Answer:	Because her boss wants her to do it.

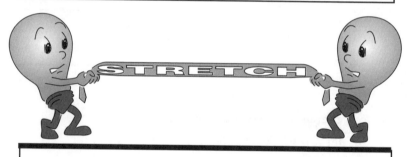

To stretch a problem, ask a chain of questions beginning with the word "what."

Example

Question:	*What is this problem about?*
Answer:	Learning financial analysis.
Question:	*What is financial analysis all about?*
Answer:	Accounting and relationships among accounts.
Question:	*What is learning all about?*
Answer:	Discovery, developing, etc.
Question:	*What is accounting all about?*
Answer:	Giving meaning to the transactions of an organization.

Stretching a problem allows you to see how much there really is to it and what other facts relate to it.

To squeeze a problem, ask a chain of questions beginning with the word "why."

Continue with these processes until you have a better understanding of the problems.

23/10. WHAT DO YOU KNOW?

Once you recognize that a problem exists, simply writing down what you know about it might help. List all the characteristics of the situation. What suspicions do you have? What kind of evidence do you have to justify those suspicions, and how good is it? What did you learn?

24/11. WHAT PATTERNS EXIST?

Look at the available information. Do you see any patterns or relationships, causal or otherwise? Draw a diagram showing the interconnections among the facts you have uncovered. Japanese managers frequently use diagrams to discuss problems. Their use of visual aids often helps them simplify complex situations. Visual representations help stimulate not only insight but creativity as well. So give diagrams a try.

25/12. THE WHY-WHY DIAGRAM

This technique is a variation of the approach used in the fishbone diagram. It is used to identify the cause(s) of a problem in a systematic way.[21] This diagram generally moves from left to right, with the problem statement on the left-hand side. (See Figure 3.2 for an abbreviated example of a why-why diagram.) There is no backbone; instead, this diagram is designed more like a traditional decision tree with component stems identified to the right of the problem statement. Branches may also be identified to the right of each stem. One moves from the problem statement to the stems and branches by asking the question "Why?"

WHY?
WHY?

Figure 3.2 Why-Why Diagram

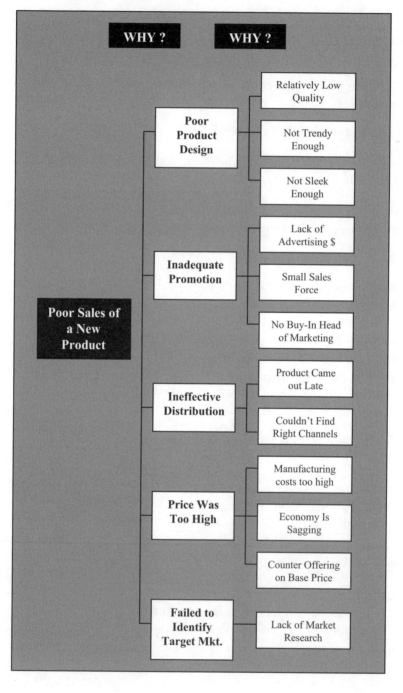

For example, as shown in Figure 3.2, if the problem is "New Product Sales Are Poor" and you ask why, five possible causes emerge: poor product design, inadequate promotion, ineffective distribution, too high a price, and failure to identify target market. Possible causes of each of these can be identified by the question "Why?" again. For example, a poor product design may be due to low quality, failure to recognize trends in consumer tastes, or aesthetic factors ("not sleek enough").

This technique offers many of the same benefits as the fishbone diagram. In particular, it helps problem solvers explore many more possible causes and relate them to the overall problem, rather than focusing on a single narrow cause. In fact, the why-why diagram probably leads to a more thorough analysis than does the fishbone diagram. Notice the differences between Figures 3.1 and 3.2. The latter is a more rational layout of problems along the more traditional lines of the marketing mix-product, promotion, price, distribution, and target market.

SUMMARY OF STEPS

1. State the problem on the left side of the paper.

2. Create a typical decision tree of causes to the right of the problem by asking a succession of "whys" regarding the prob lem and each of the possible causes.

3. Continue this process until a sufficient level of detail has been achieved.

PROBLEM STATEMENT

At the end of the problem identification stage, by using the various techniques described here, in addition to more traditional analytical approaches, you should have identified the causal problem and be able to make a more accurate problem statement than you might have otherwise.

CHAPTER

3

Various approaches to stating the problem exist. Generally, the more specific the problem can be stated, the easier it will be to solve that problem. Thus if the problem in Figure 3.2 is stated as "poor product partly due to poor quality" this would not be as effective as if the problem were stated as "poor quality due to poor workmanship caused by poor worker training."[22] Some CPS authors believe that the problem should always be stated in terms of the preposition "to," followed by some object and an action verb. An example would be, "to improve worker training on chip making machines in order to improve product quality to satisfactory levels."

TECHNIQUES FOR MAKING ASSUMPTIONS

Assumptions about the future underlie every decision you make. Assumptions set constraints on your solutions. People frequently force solutions into the shape they want by manipulating the underlying assumptions. One man entered the restaurant business after hours of spreadsheet manipulations, assuming that the revenues would be sufficient to justify the investment. Two years later he was out of business. His assumptions about sales were wrong, as were his assumptions about food costs and his own ability to motivate low-wage workers.

I know of only one creative technique for making assumptions. It's called assumption reversal.

26/1. ASSUMPTION REVERSAL

List all your assumptions about the problem. Now reverse them and try to solve the problem.[23] You aren't looking for a real solution to the newly stated problem so much as you are trying to recognize the limitations of the solutions you come up with when you use your original assumptions.

You can also use this process to get new ideas for solving the original problem. Sometimes you can use it just to get new ideas.

Suppose that your problem is to gain additional market share. The original assumptions are that another firm is dominant, you can buy market share through advertising, and you have a superior product or service that no one really knows about.

Now reverse those assumptions. No firm is dominant, advertising doesn't seem to help, and you have an inferior product that everybody knows is inferior. What are you going to do?

It's obvious that your responses to the second set of assumptions will differ from your responses to the first set. What new solutions do you come up with? In what ways can these be applied to the original problem?

Give it a try.

ANALYZING THE ENVIRONMENT, RECOGNIZING AND IDENTIFYING THE PROBLEM

The techniques listed in this chapter are some of the more creative approaches to these three stages of problem solving. Many are specifically designed to enhance creativity in these stages. The importance of creative activity in these stages is demonstrated by the example described in Creative Edge in Action 3.2.

CREATIVE EDGE IN ACTION 3.2

When Ed Zander became CEO of Motorola, he took over a company that at one time had held 50% of the global market share for cell phones. And as he soon learned, it had more reason to be proud of its past than its present. Zander's predecessor, a grandson of the founder, had sowed the seeds for a turnaround through focusing on hipper products, cost cutting and spinning off the company's capital intensive semiconductor business. Zander had to decide what the key problems were, make some assumptions about what the future would be like, and then take strong and decisive action.

One of Zander's first diagnoses was that the company had an attitude problem. People were resigned to their fate. "I had to get people to believe we could win." he says. To do this he held town meetings and small group discussions throughout the company's many locations explaining his thoughts about the future and conveying his support for the actions taken by his predecessor.

He also thought the company needed to think in terms of creating iconic products-must have products-and to do so, they had to be "cool." Zander recognized early on that the company was on the right track in product development. Referring to the company's current iconic product, the RAZR cellphone, he says, "I bumped into this thing a year ago April, and I thought it was cool." He started carrying a model of it around with him and when people saw it they would say, "I gotta have it." Right away he recognized a real opportunity for the firm and rushed the product to market.

Motorola developed a clever and creative advertising campaign for the RAZR, and despite its hefty price, it became a huge success for the company. The power of design was once again demonstrated. ("Hello Moto") Interestingly, the RAZR's design came from engineers and designers who wanted a cool product, and not from the traditional customer focus groups that Motorola typically used to develop new products.

He also took actions to push more hip products through the new product pipeline and to change the company's staid image through clever advertising. Now he is working on the company's culture, trying not to radically change it, but to steadily move it in the direction of becoming a high performance company. Zander recognizes that he can not move too fast.

"The question is how fast do you step on the gas petal? I always want to go a hundred miles an hour. But you can blow the engine on a car if you drive that fast. There are days I know I can only go fifty or sixty."

Finally, he says, "I think we ought to get back to putting the customer first. As simple as that sounds, I think it's some-thing that every American corporation, every corporation around the world, sometimes takes for granted."

Sources: Christopher Rhoads, "Motorola's Modern-izer," *Wall Street Journal* (June 23, 2005), pp. B1, B5; Ted C. Fishman, "How Ed Zander Hone RAZR's Edge," *Business 2.0* (June 2005), pp. 47-49.

In Ed Zander's actions, we see critical problem recognition (some of it quite intuitive), problem identification, and the making of critical assumptions about the future.

REFERENCES

[1] Chris Bogan, "Steal this Strategy," *Inc.* (July 2001), pp. 62-69; Thomas A. Stewart, "GE Keeps Those Ideas Coming," *Fortune* (August 12, 1991), pp. 41–49

[2] Amelia H. Ylagan, "Corporate Watch," *Business World* (November 15, 2004), p. 1.

[3] Peter T. Johnson, "Why I Race Against Phantom Competitors," *Harvard Business Review* (September/October 1988), pp. 106–112.

[4] Elicet Cruz Jimenez, et. al., "Detecting New Technologies: the Biomaterial Case," *Competitive Intelligence Magazine* (November-December 2004), pp. 23-28.

[5] William F. Pounds, "The Process of Problem Finding," *Industrial Management Review*, Fall 1969, pp. 1-9.

[6] Paul Krill, "IBM Details New Tools," *InfoWorld* (May 30, 2005), p. 19.

[7] Kent Seltzman, an MBA student of mine, suggested this process and limericks and parodies which follow.

[8] Tony Husch and Linda Foust, *That's a Great Idea*, (Berkeley, CA: 10 Speed Press, 1987).

[9] James M. Higgins and Julian W. Vincze, *Strategic Management: Text and Cases, 5th ed.*, (Ft. Worth, Tex.: The Dryden Press, 1993), Chapter 10.

[10] Arthur B. VanGundy, "The Product Improvement Checklist" (PICL™) (Point Pleasant, N.J.: Point Publishing, 1985).

[11] "Creative Group Techniques," *Small Business Report* (September 1984), pp. 52-57.

[12] Anne Skagen, "Creativity Tools: Versatile Problem Solvers That Can Double as Fun and Games," *Supervisory Management* (October 1991), pp. 1–2.

[13] No author, "The Invention of Velcro," found at Http://inventors.about.com/library/weekly/aa091207, on 8-11-05; Victor Kiam, speech to the Roy E. Crummer Graduate School of Business, Rollins College, Winter Park, Florida (October 28, 1985).

[14] Susan J. Wells, "From Ideas to Results," *HR Magazine* (February 2005), pp. 54-58.

[15] Jill Jusko, "Sharing the Wealth," *Industry Week* (November 2004), p. 63; Robert H. Schaffer and Matthew K. McCreight, "Build Your Own Change Model," *Business Horizons* (May-June 2004), pp. 63-68; Thomas A. Stewart, loc. cit.

[16] Charles Kepner and Benjamin Tregoe, *The Rational Manager*, (New York: McGraw-Hill, 1967).

[17] Bryan W. Mattimore, "Brainstormer's Boot Camp," *Success* (October 1991), pp. 22, 24.

[18] For a current discussion of Fishbone and a derivative version, see Nigel Wood, "Make It Flow: Moving from Batch and Queue to Single Piece Flow," *Management Services* (May 2004), pp. 14-18; the history of fishbone is described in Simon Majaro, *The Creative Gap: Managing Ideas for Profit* (London: Longman, 1988) pp. 133-137.

[19] Dan Koberg and Jim Bagnall, *Universal Traveler* (Los Altos, CA: William Kaufman, Inc., 1974), p. 57.

[20] Ibid., p. 63.

[21] Simon Majaro, op. cit.; pp. 137 - 138.

[22] Ibid., p. 139.

[23] Michael Michalko, Thinkertoys (Berkeley, CA: Ten Speed Press, 1992).

INDIVIDUAL TECHNIQUES
FOR
GENERATING ALTERNATIVES

An idea is salvation by imagination.
Frank Lloyd Wright

Thousands of firms such as Campbell's, Disney, General Electric, ICI, Lockheed, 3M, Pepsi, Procter & Gamble, Whirlpool, and Xerox, provide training in creativity techniques and other creativity processes, and they attribute substantial profits to their utilization by managers, professional staff, and other employees. Very importantly, research has shown that creativity training is effective and leads to increased creativity performance.[1] Companies offer such training because:

1. Successful companies are creative and innovative,[2] and creative problem solving is a core skill to those ends; and
2. One of the easiest and quickest ways of increasing the level of innovation in an organization is to develop its members' skills in creatively solving problems, especially in generating creative solutions as part of the problem-solving process.

There is nothing particularly "mystical" about these skills. People tend to think that having really good ideas is possible for only a few, and that the rest of us who don't have special "intuitive" talents cannot be creative. Nothing could be further from the truth. Being creative is innate. For most people, learning how to unleash their innate creativity is all that is needed. The techniques described in this and in other chapters help do just that. This chapter and the next one present a large number of creativity techniques for generating alternative solutions. Some may be utilized by individuals, others by work groups, most by both.

These techniques will produce results quickly and easily for virtually anyone who is willing to take the time to learn them and use them. When applied to problem solving within an appropriate organizational culture, these techniques can help an organization solve its problems more effectively than its competitors, including the problem of how to obtain a competitive advantage.

A positive feature of most of the techniques described in this chapter is their appeal to individuals with an analytical bent as well as to those with an intuitive orientation. Most of these processes rely on step-by-step procedures that fit readily into the rational problem-solving models used by most managers, professional staff, and other organizational problem solvers. Even those that at first seem entirely intuitive, such as the excursion technique (one of my ten favorite processes), when practiced by analytically as well as intuitively oriented people, will quickly reveal their value.

Every individual is likely to feel more comfortable with certain techniques than with others. In part this stems from the types of problems that a person faces most frequently and is also a function of personality characteristics such as problem-solving style. For example, I have used the following eight processes from this chapter (both personally and with clients) much more than the others (three are different from first edition of this book). But I have used almost all of them at one time or another:

Your personal preferences and problem-solving situations will help guide your choices. Table 4.3, at the end of the chapter, contains a quick guide to my favorite individual and group alternative generation processes.

INDIVIDUAL PROCESSES FOR GENERATING CREATIVE ALTERNATIVES

This chapter describes thirty-eight processes that can be used by individuals to generate creative alternatives. Some of these techniques can be used by groups as well. However, Chapter 5 describes the major techniques that can be used by groups, some of which can also be used by individuals. Most of the processes described in these two chapters can be used in various situations, but a few are appropriate only for specific types of problems. Descriptions of the more frequently used processes note such limitations where they exist.

27/1. ANALOGIES AND METAPHORS

Analogies and metaphors can serve as a means of identifying problems and understanding them better. They may also be used to generate alternative solutions. Often you can draw

CHAPTER
4

an analogy between your problem and something else, or express it in metaphorical terms. These may provide insight into how to solve the problem.

Analogies

An analogy is a comparison of two things that are essentially dissimilar but are shown through the analogy to have some similarity. Analogies are often used to solve problems. For example, two Scottish researchers, using the "Darwinian principles of evolution," created a software program to aid crime victims in identifying perpetrators. Instead of piecing together parts of the face as is traditionally done, whole faces are provided to the victims for their identification purposes. Several that "look like" the perpetrator are chosen by the victim, and then a computer program merges these faces imitating genetic selection until the best choice emerges.[3] Similarly, General Electric developed the geometry of the jet engine turbine used on Boeing's 777 airplanes using the principles of genetic evolution.[4] And, when NASA found it necessary to design a satellite that would be tethered to a space station by a thin wire sixty miles long, it realized that the motion of reeling it in would cause it to act like a pendulum with an ever-widening arc. Stanford scientist Thomas Kane, using the analogy of a yo-yo, determined that a small electric motor on the satellite would allow it to crawl back up the tether to the space station.[5] A product development team from Atlas Copco Roc Tee, a mining-equipment company based in Golden Colorado, used analogies to develop a conveyor belt. One of the members of the problem-solving team was an entomologist. He suggested the praying mantis as an example. As it eats, it clutches food between its forelegs and thrusts it into its mouth. The result of this analogy was the ROC 302, a large tractor with shovels on each side (like forelegs) that load ore onto a conveyor belt running through the middle of the machine.[6] As these examples demonstrate, while in its simplest form an analogy is a comparison of dissimilar entities, in many instances analogies are fully developed comparisons, more intricate and detailed than a metaphor or a simile. Using them often leads to increased levels of creativity.

Metaphors

A metaphor is a figure of speech in which two different universes of thought are linked by some point of similarity. In the broadest sense of the term, all metaphors are simple analogies, but not all analogies are metaphors. Typically, metaphors treat one thing as if it were something else so that a resemblance that would not ordinarily be perceived is pointed out. Examples include *the idea drought, frozen wages, the corporate battleground,* and *liquid assets.* Also: The sergeant *barks* an order, the cold wind *cuts* to the bone, and the road was a *ribbon* of moonlight. Metaphors have many uses in creative endeavors. For example, they have been used in sales to create new ways of viewing old realities.[7]

Hiroo Wantanabe, a project team leader for Honda, coined the following metaphor to describe his team's tremendous challenge: The Theory of Automobile Evolution, 'If a car could indeed evolve like a living organism, how should it evolve?' he asked his team. This thought process eventually led them to a very successful car model.[8] And when Gap decided to launch a new design for the display areas in its Colorado stores, one which would cater to older, more upscale customers, it chose an art gallery theme. "The in-store experience and emotion a customer feels are important. We need to be a part of that," said Christopher Hufnagel, Gap's vice president of brand store experience. "Our metaphor was an art gallery. It's clean and plain with amazing lighting and simple classic features. Our art is our product."[9]

Comparisons that are obvious are not metaphors. To say that the noise of firecrackers on the Fourth of July sounds like gunfire, for example, is not a metaphor. Metaphors occur when a surprisingly imaginative connection is made between two different ideas or images that are normally perceived as dissimilar.

Think of five metaphors that describe the meaning of life, such as "life is a maze."

1. _____

2. _____

3. _____

4. _____

5. _____

Now think of a problem. Write five metaphors that describe your problem.

1. _____

2. _____

3. _____

4. _____

5. _____

For each of the metaphors you have listed, ask yourself what insights it provides into how to solve your problem. What solutions do your metaphors suggest?

SUMMARY OF STEPS

1. Think of an analogy between your problem and something else.
2. Ask yourself what insights or potential solutions the analogy suggests.

28/2. ANALYSIS OF PAST SOLUTIONS; AND LEARNING FROM FAILURES

Technical reports, professional reports, and books and articles telling how others have solved problems can be employed to determine possible solutions for a problem. Even if the ways in which problems have been solved in the past are not exactly suited to your situation, you can adapt them on the basis of your own experience. And analyzing your own successes and those of others, and sharing that knowledge is part and parcel of the techniques of benchmarking and best practices mentioned earlier.

But some firms, for example, Eli Lilly, the pharmaceutical giant, learn from their mistakes and often turn them into successes. When a drug fails, commercially or medically, Lilly assigns a team of consultants, doctors and researchers to find out what went wrong and why. It is often able to save a drug or through the creative generation of alternative uses, is often able to turn a failed drug in one area of medicine into a success in another, usually related area of medicine. Lilly successes such as Alimta, which is used in the treatment of mesothelioma, a rare type of cancer caused by exposure to asbestos, and Evista, a $1 billion a year drug for osteoporosis, began their commercial lives at Lilly as failures. With Alimta, changes in the drug made in successful for its originally targeted malady, while Evista began its life as a contraceptive. Why treat failures as dead ends, why not try and profit from them? This approach is about corporate mind set.[10]

29/3. ASSOCIATION

Association involves making a mental connection between two objects or ideas. It works through three primary laws originally laid down by the ancient Greeks: contiguity, similarity, and contrast.[11] *Contiguity* means nearness—for example, when you see a chalkboard you are reminded of school. *Similarity* means that one object or thought will remind you of a similar object or thought. For example, when you see a Nissan Maxima you might think of a Nissan 350 ZX. Metaphors and analogies depend on similarity. *Contrast* refers to dissimilarities that are nearly opposites—black/white, man/woman, child/adult. Thus, association involves thinking of something near, similar to, or in contrast to the object or idea in question. Much of creativity is about making associations.[12] Free association is one technique for doing that.

Free Association

In free association, you say whatever comes into your mind relative to a word you just wrote or relative to a one- or two-word definition of a problem. A trail of thoughts is pursued in this way. Free association is a good group exercise as well as an individual one. The purpose is simply to get thoughts onto a whiteboard or sheet of paper that will trigger new thoughts about the problem. You don't expect to find solutions per se; rather, you are looking for thoughts that might lead to solutions. For example, on one occasion a group of bank managers started free associating on the word "fast." "Fox" and "jet plane" were among the associations that resulted; so was "Federal Express." "Federal Express," in turn, led the group to think of bar codes and optical scanners, which were perceived as a possible solution to the problem: differentiating among home equity loans. The bar codes could be used to inform customers of the status of the loan at any point in the approval process. Later the bank instituted 24-hour approvals for home equity loans, which left this solution without a problem, but the free-association technique had been used effectively.

At Campbell Soup Company, product developers began by randomly selecting the word "handle" from a dictionary. (Organized random search is described later in this chapter.) Through free association the word "utensil" was suggested. This led to "fork." One participant joked about a soup that could be eaten with a fork. The group reasoned that you couldn't eat soup with a fork unless it was thick with vegetables and meat ... and Campbell's Chunky Soups, an extremely successful product line, was born.[13]

Now try free associating, starting with a one-word summary of your problem on line 1. On line 2, write down the first word that comes to mind after looking at line 1. On line 3, write down the first word that comes to mind after looking at line 2. Continue until you have twenty words.

1. _____

2. _____

3. _____

4. _____

5. _____

6. _____

7. _____

8. _____

9. _____

10. _____

11. _____

12. _____

13. _____

14. _____

15. _____

16. _____

17. _____

18. _____

19. _____

20. _____

Creativity consultant Roger von Oech used names of celebrities to trigger ideas. The problem was to develop icons for a new software package. When Vanna White's name was introduced, the group thought first of letter turning, then pretty women, and finally, for some reason, airhead. Bingo! The new icon was a vacuum cleaner for a function that collected something from one place and put it somewhere else.[14]

Regular Association

The difference between free association and regular association is that in regular association, the associated word must somehow be related to the word before it. Thus, "airplane" could lead to "pilot" but not to "tree." In free association, in contrast, any word, the first word that pops into your mind, can be used.

SUMMARY OF STEPS

1. Write down a word (or two) that may or may not represent your problem or some aspect of it.
2. Write down whatever word comes to mind relative to this word.
3. After completing a series of such associations, study the words to see if any of them lead to insights or solutions to your problem.

30/4. ATTRIBUTE ASSOCIATION CHAINS

As in attribute listing, this technique begins with a list of the attributes of a problem. But instead of analytically changing the attributes as you would in attribute listing, you free associate on each attribute to generate ideas about the problem.[9]

For example, suppose that the problem is to improve on the generic MP3 as a device for carrying and playing music. You begin by listing the attributes of the MP3—its memory size, weight, color, composition, cost, design, and so on. If you free associated on these attributes, you might look for ways to reduce the weight of the device or cut its cost or change its composition. If you free associated on "cool looks" you might come up with words like: "bright colors," "change," "lasers," "mouse," and so on. Eventually, you might have developed the iPod. Now think size and then really small—and you have the iPod nano.

Like many of the techniques discussed in this book, this one depends on your ability to let your mind go (in this case, to free associate) and to come up with ideas based on thoughts that are seemingly unrelated. You have to be able to envision how the results might be applied to the problem. For example, in the case of MP3 devices for carrying music, you need to be able to envision how the application of "color" or "mouse" would lead to a "cool looking" device.

SUMMARY OF STEPS

1. List all the attributes or qualities of a problem or object.
2. Free associate on each attribute or group of attributes and attempt to generate solutions to or insights into the problem or object.
3. Study the suggested solutions to determine which one is feasible.
4. Examine the remaining associated words to determine what solutions they suggest, and then determine which of these is most feasible.

31/5. ATTRIBUTE LISTING

The technique of attribute listing, developed by Professor Robert Platt Crawford of the University of Nebraska, consists of listing all the attributes or qualities of a problem, object, (or product, service, or process).[16] Then the problem solver systematically analyzes each attribute or group of attributes and attempts to change them in as many ways as possible. Examples of attributes include physical attributes, such as color, speed, odor, weight, size, and mass; social attributes, such as norms, taboos, responsibilities, leadership, and communication; psychological attributes, such as perception, motivation, appearance, symbolism, self-image, and needs; and other attributes such as cost, function, length of service, and so on.

For example, if you chose to improve on services provided in a hospital emergency room, you might observe an ER for a period of time, making a list of all of the events that took place, their durations and their frequencies. Then you would have a list of the attributes/components of this customer experience and other important pieces of information. This is precisely what Fred Dust, head of IDEO's Smart Spaces practices did for their client Kaiser Permanente. Many of his observations led immediately to solu-tions. In one instance, he found that one major problem with the customer experience was that patients were extremely anxious about when they would be seen by a doctor. A simple television monitor in the waiting room that indicated the order in which would be seen was, for Fred, an obvious solution.[17]

SUMMARY OF STEPS

1. List all the attributes or qualities of a problem or object.
2. Systematically analyze each attribute or group of attributes and attempt to change it in as many ways as possible.
3. Review the resulting attributes for the best solutions.

32/6 BACK TO THE CUSTOMER

Turning our attention from production problems to market-ing problems, we can consider how what we do relates to the customer in terms of product, price, promotion, distri-bution, target market and customer experience. As an exer-cise, below each of the following headings write the key re-lated issues you should consider in going "back to the cus-tomer" to solve your problem. This means that you would identify issues for each of the six marketing mix factors re-lated to the problem. Then identify solutions for each of these issues.

PRODUCT: _____

_____

_____

_____

PRICE: _____

_____

_____

_____

PROMOTION: _____

_____

_____

_____

DISTRIBUTION: _____

_____

_____

_____

TARGET MARKET:_____

_____

_____

_____

CUSTOMER EXPERIENCE: _____

_____

_____

_____

What insights did you gain? Do any of your entries remind
you of something else? Do they lead to any new ideas?

SUMMARY OF STEPS

1. State your problem.
2. Identify the various product, price, promotion, distribution, target market, and customer experience issues related to solving that
   problem in terms of how the customer would be affected.

33/7. BACK TO THE SUN

All physical things can be reduced to their energy equivalents. By tracing their history back to the natural resources from which they were developed, and ultimately to the sun as the source of all energy, we can better appreciate how the elements of a problem are related.[18] This better understanding may suggest solutions.

Suppose, for example, that we are trying to develop a shoe using different materials than those commonly used, or a different way of using existing materials in making shoes. When you look at a shoe you see leather, rubber, strings, nails, polish, thread, and so on. For each of these elements you can trace a process back to natural resources and ultimately to the sun.

RUBBER: stamps, mold, heel factories, shipping, raw latex process, rubber plant, rubber tree.

STRINGS: plastic tips, woven fabric, coloring, fiber, woven fiber, spun fiber, drawn fiber, plastic, petroleum, chemicals, fossil deposits.

LEATHER: texturing, coloring, hole punching, cutting out, tannery, slaughterhouse, trucking, ranch, feed.

POLISH: application, coloring, container, mixing, trucking, petroleum, chemicals, fossil deposits.

NAILS: hammer, forge, wire, spools, steel, Pittsburgh shipping, Minnesota iron, ore deposits.

Do any of these words suggest new materials or uses? For example, could rubber be stamped differently, colored differently? Could different fibers be used? Could strings be all plastic, not cloth, or made of something besides cloth or plastic? Could leather be made from something besides cowhide? Could the leather be a different color? Could polish be made from something other than chemicals? Looking at these words may trigger new thoughts.

34/8. CIRCLE OF OPPORTUNITY

This process consists of randomly selecting problem attributes and combining them to create a topic for a brainstorming session.[19] This process can be time-consuming but very rewarding in terms of ideas generated. The technique is somewhat similar to the attribute-listing and attribute association processes discussed previously, although it

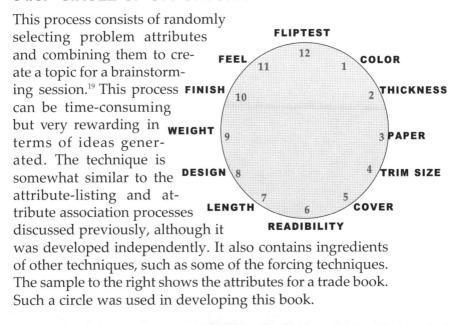

was developed independently. It also contains ingredients of other techniques, such as some of the forcing techniques. The sample to the right shows the attributes for a trade book. Such a circle was used in developing this book.

SUMMARY OF STEPS

1. Define the problem–for example, developing a new product or refining an old one.
2. Draw a circle and number it like a clock from 1 to 12.
3. Select any twelve attributes of the problem (e.g., of the product or service) and list these in positions 1 to 12 on the "clockface."
4. Throw a die or dice to determine the number of the first attribute to be worked on.
5. Individually or in a group, brainstorm, free associate, and/or mind map whatever thoughts about that attribute occur to you.
6. Continue rolling the dice until you have used all twelve numbers and worked on all of the attributes.
7. Make combinations of attributes, either by arbitrarily choosing combinations or by rolling the dice. Now brainstorm, free associate, and/or mind map those combinations.

35/9. COMPUTER PROGRAMS

There are numerous software programs that can be used to generate alternatives and otherwise add creativity to the problem-solving process. Several of these follow:

- The best known of these is probably "Mind-Manager®" from MindJet which can be found at MindJet.com. As its name suggests, it is a mind mapping software (see technique #46/20 in this chapter) based on the works of Tony Buzan. It is a very easy to use program and great for using with groups via a laptop projector.
- Another well known and computationally powerful program is "IdeaFisher®" from Fisher Idea Systems. This program contains 60,000 words and phrases together with 650,000 idea-associations that are linked to several thousand questions. The questions are grouped into three divisions: (1) orientation-clarification, (2) modification, and (3) evaluation. The questions provoke ideas and associations that can be used to solve common business problems.[20] It costs around $400.
- "Idea Generator Plus" is another program that can be used in solving problems. It focuses mainly on walking the problem-solver through the problem solving process, making sure that all aspects of the problem have been considered. It can also be used to generate alternatives.[21]
- "Mindlink" uses a series of mind triggers to assist problem solving. It asks the user to abandon normal association processes and go for the unusual. For example, it may ask you to link an elephant with an oil well, and then determine how this association might give clues to solving your problem. "Mindlink" opens with a set of creativity warm-up exercises known as The Gym. Other sections include Idea Generation, Guided Problem Solving, and General Problem Solving.[22]
- "IdeaPro" is part of "Serious Creativity" a creativity training package from Edward de Bono, the creator of "lateral thinking" and "Six Thinking Hats." IdeaPro is a tool for creating and developing new ideas.
- "Brainstormer" guides the brainstorming process, provides idea triggers, and ranks ideas for a group.
- Finally, "The Invention Machine" uses problem definition questions, a database of 1250 types of engineering problems, a database of 1230 scientific effects (e.g., physical or chemical), and examples of 2000 of the world's most innovative inventions to offer suggestions

on solving your problem. Russian engineer Michael Valdman used this program to redesign pizza boxes. The program suggested changes in shapes and materials that led to a box that keeps pizza warm three times as long as conventional boxes.[23] This program is based on TRIZ. (see technique 61/35 in this chapter.)

All of these programs can be found on the Internet.
And one of the best things about all of these, except The Invention Machine, is that there are brief, free trial programs for them.

36/10. DEADLINES

Many creative individuals claim that they work best under pressure. Deadlines then would appear to be extremely effective in generating alternatives and inspiring creative work. A deadline increases pressure and for many this stimulates more right-brain activity. Researcher Teresa Amabile, however, has shown that at least for those she studied, the greatest levels of creativity do not follow time pressures but periods of relaxation.[24]

37/11. DIRECT ANALOGIES

In a direct analogy facts, knowledge, or technology from one field are applied to another. Biology is a fertile field for such analogies. A few years ago a manufacturer of potato chips was faced with a frequently encountered problem: Potato chips took up too much space on the shelf when they were packed loosely, but they crumbled when they were packed in smaller packages. The manufacturer found a solution by using a direct analogy. What naturally occurring object is similar to a potato chip? How about dried leaves? Dried leaves crumble very easily, however, and are bulky. The analogy was a good one. What about pressed leaves? They're flat. Could potato chips somehow be shipped flat, or nearly flat? Unfortunately, the problem of crumbling remained. Continuing the creative process, the decision makers realized that leaves are not pressed while they are dry but while they are moist. They determined

CHAPTER
4

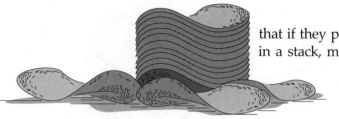

that if they packed potato chips in a stack, moist enough not to crumble but dry enough to be flat, or nearly flat, they might just solve the problem. The result, as you may have guessed, was Pringle's.[25]

Scientists and engineers at Oregon State University have examined spiders and other bugs in an attempt to improve the agility of robots. According to one of the researchers, Eugene F. Fichter, "They're magnificent models for walking machines." Insects and spiders are filmed and their motions analyzed by computers to see whether they can be emulated by much heavier robots. A farm products company seeking a way of planting seeds at exactly the same distance apart used a machinegun belt as an analogy. The firm created a biodegradable tape studded with equally spaced seeds that could be laid in a furrow.[26]

When Dupont researchers were trying to develop a fire-resistant Nomex fiber that could be dyed without requiring special procedures, they were stumped because the fiber's tight structure made it impossible for dye to adhere to it. Then one of the researchers asked how miners could go into coal mines. The answer was that props kept the mine from collapsing. Applying this analogy, he embedded a large organic molecule in the fiber during manufacturing. This molecule dug a hole and propped it open so that dye could be applied. One result of this innovation was the widespread use of flame-resistant Nomex in aircraft interiors.[27] Don't forget that sometimes discovering direct analogies happens by accident, and not the result of research. Creative Edge in Action 4.1 describes how "biomimicry"—biologically inspired design—which uses direct analogies from nature to develop new products is taking industry by storm.

Nature's Design Workshop

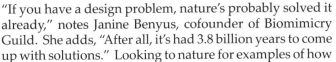

"If you have a design problem, nature's probably solved it already," notes Janine Benyus, cofounder of Biomimicry Guild. She adds, "After all, it's had 3.8 billion years to come up with solutions." Looking to nature for examples of how to design materials and even processes, is enabling scientists to better design products for human beings ranging from desalinating water to streamlining cars.

For example, Jewel beetles, which lay their eggs in recently burned trees, can detect fires from miles away. The defense industry is studying how these beetles accomplish this; seeking clues for low-cost heat detectors with military applicability. Similarly, Volvo is researching locusts' ability to fly in dense swarms without colliding. Volvo hopes to find a possible key to avoiding collisions among cars. NASA supported researchers at Princeton are analyzing the remarkable strength of abalone shells in search of impact-resistant coatings for thermal tiles. Using the same principle that geckos use to walk up the sides of walls, the Defense Advanced Research Projects Agency (DARPA) is developing a robot that can climb vertical surfaces. Why? "Imagine a Mars rover that's not limited to flat terrain," says biologist Keller Autumn of Lewis & Clark College, who is working with DARPA on this project. In all of these cases, direct analogies are being applied. Find out what works in nature, and although it may take some radical adaptation, make it work in industry.

Even items we already use every day may benefit from biomimicry. You know how the screens on laptops and digital cameras tend to fade or wash out in bright light. The key to solving this problem may lie with the brilliance we see in peacock feathers. It's not what you think. It isn't the pigments in peacock feathers that give them their iridescent blue and green colors. The only actual pigment in these feathers is brown. It is the repeating microstructures on the feathers that reflect certain light wavelengths in perfect sync that intensify a given hue. Qualcomm is working on a color display capability that is based the same type of microstructures just behind the screen surface. Because the display depends on ambient light rather than light internally generated, the display actually becomes brighter outdoors. Ultimately, the goal is not just to design better products based on nature's designs, but also processes. For example, scientists at Sandia National Laboratories are already working on manufacturing processes that mimic how nature constructs seashells.

Source: Anne Underwood, "Nature's Design Workshop," *Newsweek* (September 26, 2005), p. 55.

CREATIVE EDGE IN ACTION 4.1

Think of a problem. Now write a direct analogy for that problem.

_____

_____

_____

What possible solutions emerge from your analogy?

A major use of analogies and comparisons in general, is the excursion technique. This technique is usually employed after more traditional approaches, such as individual or group brainstorming, or Mind mapping, have been attempted without success. Those involved put the problem aside for a while and "take an excursion" in their minds. This is essentially a word association exercise that uses visualization. A word or group of words that are colorful and have a lot of visual appeal should be used. The problem solvers spend time constructing fantasies based on the word or words chosen. Then they are asked to make a connection between their fantasies and the original problem. The "excursion" could be a trip through a natural history museum, a jungle, a zoo, or a big city. Numerous companies have used this technique successfully after other approaches have failed. The excursion technique can be used by an individual but because it is essentially a group process, it is described in Chapter 5.

SUMMARY OF STEPS

1. Find another field of science or area of endeavor that could provide an analogy to your problem.
2. Create an analogy that allows you to apply facts, knowledge, or technology from the other field to your problem
3. Determine what insights or potential solutions this analogy yields.

38/12. ESTABLISH IDEA SOURCES

To come up with ideas, I like to flip through magazines, especially *Fast Company, Wired, Business 2.0, Fortune, Business Week, Popular Science* and *The Futurist*. These all display lots of ideas in short boxed features and photos. For example, *Popular Science* always has several pages describing and picturing new products in every issue. *Business Week* has annual design and new product winner awards with photos and comments on winners; and both it and *Fast Company* have numerous features on innovation. I also keep a file of over 5,000 articles and use a PC article-research data base. If you don't have places to go for ideas, find some. Take time now to make a list of possible sources of ideas. Don't limit yourself to familiar sources; search out additional places where you can get ideas. You might start with encyclopedias, science fiction books, magazines, catalogs, movies, seminars, museums, art galleries, and amusement parks, for example. Most of these have versions on the Internet which provide lots of visual stimulation. Also, try a Google search (see technique 43/17).

39/13. EXAMINE IT WITH THE SENSES

Can you use your senses (hearing, sight, touch, smell, taste) to come up with ideas about a problem, and how to solve it? List the insights and potential solutions you think of when you ask the following questions about your problem:

1. How does it feel? _____

2. How does it smell? _____

3. How does it look? _____

4. What sound does it make? _____

5. What does it taste like? _____

Insights	Possible Solutions
1. _____	1. _____
2. _____	2. _____
3. _____	3. _____
4. _____	4. _____
5. _____	5. _____

Do your answers trigger any thoughts that might lead to motivations? Any solutions?

40/14. THE FCB GRID

If you are looking for new products or services to offer and are trying to figure out how to position them against those of competitors, this technique may help. The FCB grid was developed by Richard Vaughn of the advertising corporation of Foote, Cone & Belding.[28] It is a four-cell matrix similar to those commonly used to describe management and marketing concepts. Figure 4.1 portrays such a grid.

The two axes indicate positions of high and low involvement and degrees of thinking and feeling in relation to products and services. "High involvement" describes expensive products or services, such as automobiles, expensive jewelry, airplanes, and custom-designed software. "Low involvement" describes inexpensive products like dishwashing soap or fast food.

"Think" represents products or services that are evaluated according to verbal, numerical, analytical, and cognitive criteria, about which the consumer would desire more information or would have to think. Examples include computers, spreadsheet software, automobiles, and customized fitness programs. "Feel" describes products or services that appeal to the customer's emotions, about which the customer would have feelings. Examples include cosmetics, stylish clothing, and sports cars.

The axes are continuums with high and low involvement, and think and feel, at the extremes of the axes and different degrees of these variables in between. The idea is to place

Figure 4.1 FCB Grid

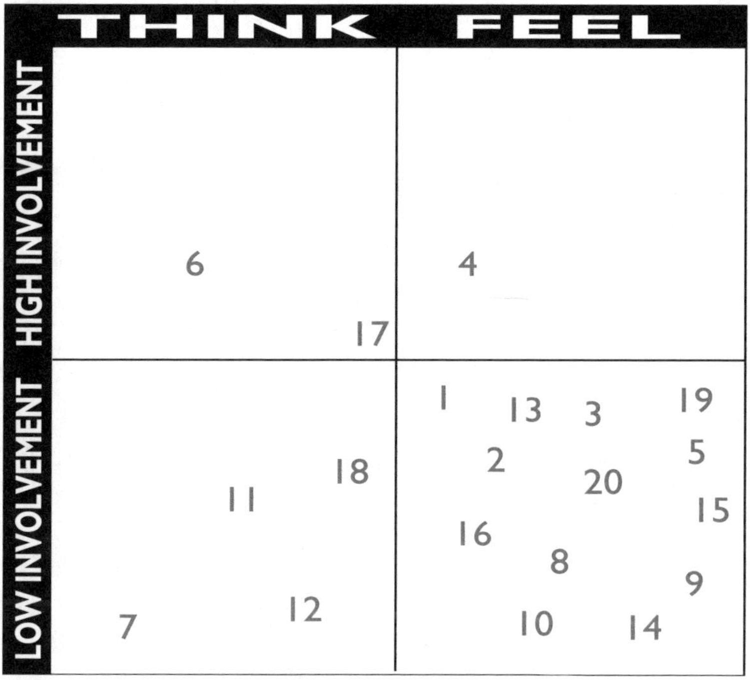

THINK	FEEL
HIGH INVOLVEMENT 6 17	4
LOW INVOLVEMENT 11 18 7 12	1 13 3 19 2 20 5 16 15 8 9 10 14

Figure 4.2 FCB Grid for Creativity Books

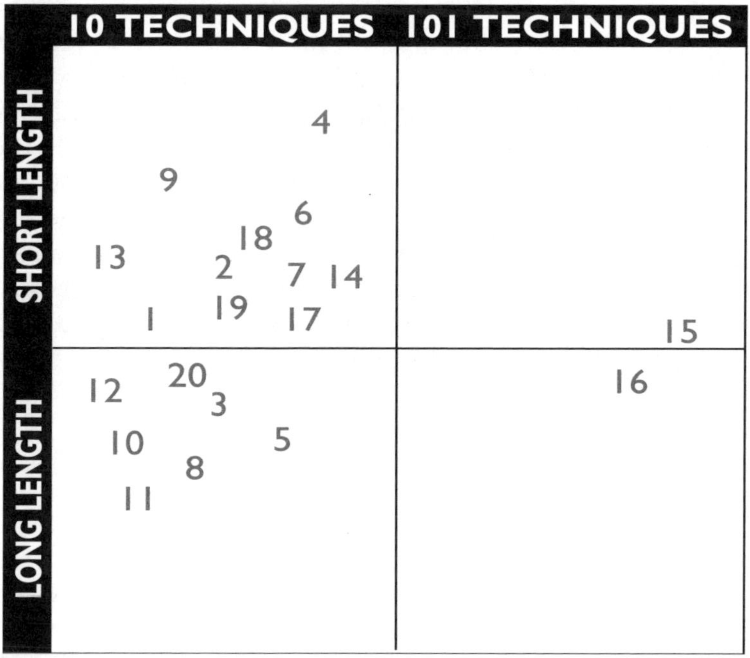

10 TECHNIQUES	101 TECHNIQUES
SHORT LENGTH 4 9 6 18 13 2 7 14 1 19 17	15
LONG LENGTH 12 20 3 10 5 8 11	16

existing products on the grid according to their characteristics and then to find the holes in the market, that is, places where competitors don't have products.

For example, if we look at all the books on creativity techniques—and there are at least twenty such books—we find that they are, with few exceptions, low involvement/feel books. This book, *101 Creative Problem Solving Techniques*, in contrast, was designed to be a medium-involvement/think and feel book. The "think" orientation is a rational choice reflecting my perception of the market for such books. It's the "hole" in the market, or at least part of it. But, I have added some feeling characteristics in order to make the book more visual, an important aspect of increasing creativity.

The beauty of the FCB grid is that you can put anything you want on the axes. Such grids are common in marketing and strategic planning analyses. For example, Michael Porter, noted consultant, researcher, and author uses a similar grid to plot the characteristics of competitors' strategies as well as those of the subject firm. Using these strategic maps, he determines where to position the subject firm relative to other firms' strategies.[29]

You can do what Porter has done, using whatever continuums are meaningful. If, for example, you place on one axis the number of creativity techniques described in books like this one, you will find 101 techniques on one end and 10 or so on the other. This book is positioned at the "101 techniques" end of that axis. (See Figure 4.2.) On the other axis you might place the length of descriptions of techniques, with long at one end and short at the other. This book mixes the lengths, but the average is somewhere between the two extremes. As this example reveals, more than one grid may be necessary to understand the desired position of a product or service in the market.

41/15. THE FOCUSED-OBJECT TECHNIQUE

The focused-object technique contains elements of both free association and forced relationships.[30] It is especially useful in situations requiring high levels of creativity, such as obtaining ideas for advertising layouts or copy. The principal difference between this technique and the other forced-relationship techniques is that one object or idea in the relationship is deliberately chosen, not selected at random.

The other object or idea is selected arbitrarily. The attributes or qualities of this second object or idea are then used as a starting point for a series of free associations. An attempt is made to adapt the resulting stream of associations to the chosen object or problem. In the case of advertising copy and art ideas, the deliberately selected object is usually the product to be advertised.

The example in Table 4.1 shows how the forced-relationship technique was used to associate with an automobile. (The automobile was the preselected object.) The attributes of the lampshade were the starting point for a chain of free associations that led to other ideas. The third column shows how the associations were applied to the problem of obtaining copy and layout ideas for the automobile.

TABLE 4.1 Application of the Focused-Object echnique		
Attribute of Lampshade	**Chain of Free Association**	**Application to Automobile**
Lampshade is shaped like a peak or volcano	Volcano Volcanic power	
	Explosive power	"Engine has explosive power."
	Peak Peak of perfection	"This automobile is the peak of perfection."
	Steep hill	"It has climbing ability."
Lampshade has form	Racing form	Use a layout.
	Horses Horsepower	Show individual horse to dramatize horsepower.
	Winner's circle Fine horses	"This automobile is always in the winner's circle."
	Other fine things Morocco leather Ivory chess sets	"He likes fine cars." Associate car with fine things.
	Africa	Picture car in use in Africa and all over the world.

Source: Charles S. Whiting, "Operational Techniques of Creative Thinking," *Advanced Management*, October 1955, p. 29.

SUMMARY OF STEPS

1. Pick a product, service, or object to change.
2. List the attributes of this item.
3. Free associate words for each attribute.
4. Indicate how each free association applies to changing the item or solving the problem at hand.

42/16 FRESH EYE

Bring in someone from the outside who doesn't know any-thing about the problem, perhaps someone from another functional area or another company. Or bring in a consult-ant, someone who is an expert on creativity but not an ex-pert in your particular field. Such a person may see the prob-lem with a fresh eye. Not being immersed in the project, the outsider may provide some new ideas. Try getting a 6-year-old to look at the problem. Children haven't been so-cialized not to be creative and will say what they think; what they think might just be right.

43/17. GOOGLESTORMING

This technique first came to my attention through Joyce Wycoff, founder and president of the Innovation Network. She sug-gests that you use your search engine to help you expand your thinking. Look around your office, your home, or around the neighborhood area and pick an item. Do a Google, Yahoo or other search engine search on that item. Then pick the first three or four, or for that matter, any three or four of the matches that come up for this item on your search engine, and then read the entries. These descriptions should help you generate new perspectives about your problem. You can continue this process endlessly for all the items that turn up as matches. Google storming is essentially an organized random—tech-nique 50/24—search by computer. As with that technique you can use the matches to create a forced choice type checklist.

44/18. IDEA BITS AND RACKING

Carl Gregory, author of *The Management of Intelligence*, sug-gests that one way of assembling "idea bits," or ideas gener-ated in individual or group sessions, is to use a specially designed "racking board."[31] The idea slips or cards contain-ing the ideas are placed on this racking board for examina-tion. To construct a racking board you need some small shelf units with grooves to hold the cards. Alternatively, a mag-netic device or tape can be used to stick cards to a board or wall. This technique is like storyboarding (described in Chapter 5), except that with idea bits you begin with pieces of unrelated information. Idea bits may be sudden flashes of insight, notes arising from conversations or readings, observations, objectives, information, ideas produced in a brainstorming session, new words or phrases, and so on. Putting them on a racking board allows you to look at them and see if there is any pattern to them.

45/19. INPUT-OUTPUT

This technique, developed by General Electric for use in its creative engineering program, helps identify new ways to accomplish an objective, as illustrated in the following example:[32]

A dynamic system can be classified according to its (1) input, (2) output, and (3) limiting requirements or specifications. For example in designing a device to automatically shade a room during bright sunlight, the problem can be defined as follows:

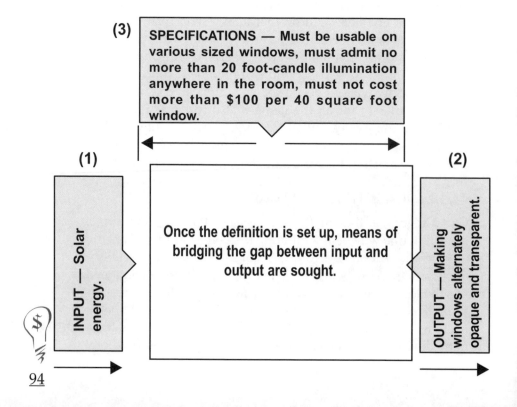

(3) SPECIFICATIONS — Must be usable on various sized windows, must admit no more than 20 foot-candle illumination anywhere in the room, must not cost more than $100 per 40 square foot window.

(1) INPUT — Solar energy.

Once the definition is set up, means of bridging the gap between input and output are sought.

(2) OUTPUT — Making windows alternately opaque and transparent.

At each step the question is asked: can this phenomenon (input) be used directly to shade the window (desired output)? Using the above example once again, we observe that solar energy is of two types, light and heat.

Step 1: What phenomena respond to application of heat? light? Are there vapors that cloud upon heating? Gases expand, metals expand, solids melt. Are there substances that cloud in bright light? Does light cause some materials to move or curl? Light causes photo-electric cells to produce current, chemicals to decompose, plants to grow.

Step 2: Can any of these phenomena be used directly to shade the window? Vapors that cloud on heating? Substances that cloud in bright light? Bi-metals warp. Slats of a blind could warp shut.

Step 3: What phenomena respond to step 1 outputs? Gases expand, could operate a bellows, etc. Photoelectric current could operate a solenoid, etc. Solids melt, effect on electric conductivity, etc.

Step 4: Can any of these phenomena be used directly to shade the window? Bellows could operate a blind, etc.

Step 5: What phenomena respond to step 3 output? Bellows, solenoid, etc., could operate a solenoid switch or valve, which in turn could operate motors to draw the blind.

In this manner a number of possible solutions can be developed for evaluation.

SUMMARY OF STEPS

1. Determine system input, desired output, and limiting requirements or specifications.
2. Brainstorm ways of bridging the gap between the input and the desired output, given the limiting requirements or specifications.
3. Use the attributes of the input to suggest solutions.
4. Continually ask the question, "Can these phenomena (attributes) lead to the desired output in any way?"
5. Evaluate the alternatives generated in this way.

46/20. MIND MAPPING

Mind mapping was originated by Tony Buzan of the Buzan Organization in England.[33]   This technique is based on research findings showing that the brain works primarily with key concepts in an interrelated and integrated manner. Whereas traditional thinking opts for columns and rows, Buzan feels that "working out" from a core idea suits the brain's thinking patterns better. The brain also needs a way to "slot in" ideas that are relevant to the core idea. To achieve these ends, Buzan developed mind mapping.

Mind mapping originated as an individual brainstorming process but is equally beneficial when used in groups. In brainstorming, you are interested in generating as many ideas as possible, even wild and crazy ones. Just write or otherwise record whatever comes into your head as it occurs. Quantity, not quality, is what you are after. No criticism is allowed during the brainstorming itself. Later you can go back and critique your inputs (or those of others in a group situation). You can also generate new ideas by looking at what you have already written— that is, "piggyback" on what has already been done. (See Chapter 5 for further discussion of this technique.)

To begin a mind mapping session, write the name or description of the object or problem in the center of a piece of paper and draw a circle around it. Then brainstorm each major facet of that object or problem, drawing lines outward from the circle like roads leaving a city. You can draw branches from those "roads" as you brainstorm them in more detail. You can brainstorm main lines at once and then the branches for each, or brainstorm a line and its branches, or jump from place to place as thoughts occur. To make the mind map more useful, you might draw each major branch extending from your central thought in a different color. As you branch out, you may notice related topics appearing on different branches. These relationships can be emphasized by circling the items in question, or drawing lines under or between them. Finally, study your mind map and look for interrelationships and terms appearing more than once. A sample mind map is shown in Figure 4.3. Joyce Wycoff's *Mind Mapping* [34] provides additional and very useful business examples of how to use this technique.

Mind mapping is an excellent technique not only for generating new ideas but also for developing one's intuitive capacity. It is especially useful for identifying all the issues and subissues related to a problem, as well as the solutions to a problem and their pros and cons. The latter is accomplished by making the main branches the solutions and the

Figure 4.3 A Sample Mind Map

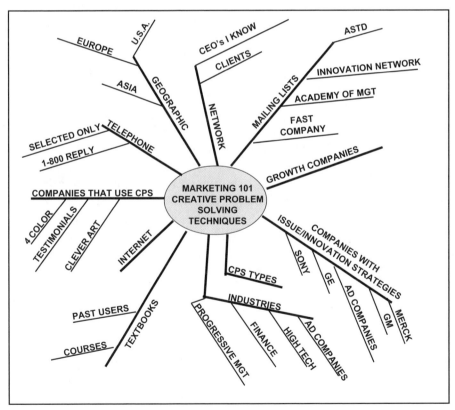

subbranches from each of these the pros and cons. Mind mapping also works well for outlining presentations, papers, and book chapters.

In fact, mind mapping can be used in a wide variety of situations. For example, mind mapping is especially useful for project management.[35] It is also extensively used in education at virtually every level from kindergarten to executive education courses. For example, it was used to teach creativity in a college marketing class.[36] The extremely successful socio/technical forecasting firm, Inferential Focus, founded by Charles Hess and Carol Coleman, uses Mind Maps® to spot trends and predict periods of change before they occur.[37] A major aerospace firm has used mind mapping to help layout the project plan for a major strategic change initiative.[38] And when Michael Stanley was the engineer in charge of Boeing's technical publications unit, he used Mind Maps® extensively. He even kept a spiral notebook of Mind Maps® covering the "basic subjects that I've got to know to do my job." He also had a 40 x 4 foot Mind Map® on his wall that he used to show top management about a new process he had designed for developing technical publications.[39]

In my experience, about half of the people who learn this process find it extremely useful; the other half find it uncomfortable to use. The latter seem to object to the lack of structure and find it difficult to be as spontaneous as the process requires. But for those who are comfortable with it, it can be a very useful and versatile tool. As author Jill Neimark notes, "Once you've got the knack of letting your mind flow onto this visual chessboard (a Mind Map®), you can apply it to anything from business to relationships to your future."[40]

There are two mind mapping software programs of which I am aware: MindManager® which is sold by Mindjet Corporation and can be found at Mindjet.com; and MindGenius® which is sold by Gael Ltd and can be found at MindGenius.com. I have used MindManager® extensively and found it to be excellent for a host of uses. It has over 500,000 licensees according to its Web site. It is effective for personal use on your laptop or PC, and equally effective for group brainstorming and problem solving activity using a projector system. I have only recently become aware of MindGenius®. It appears to have similar features to those found with MindManager®.

SUMMARY OF STEPS

1. Write the name or description of the object or problem in the center of a piece of paper and draw a circle around it.
2. Brainstorm each major facet of that object or problem, placing your thoughts on lines drawn outward from the central thought like roads leaving a city.
3. Add branches to the lines as necessary.
4. Use additional visual techniques–for example, different colors for major lines of thought, circles around words or thoughts that appear more than once, connecting lines between similar thoughts.
5. Study the mind map to see what interrelationships exist and what solutions are suggested.

47/21. MUSIC

Listening to soft, calming music is a good way to "free up" your subconscious. Music is listened to on the right side of the brain, the more intuitive side (for right-handed people). Music also tends to put the analytical side of the brain to sleep, allowing the intuitive side to become more active.[41]

48/22. NAME POSSIBLE USES

Naming the possible uses for an item helps provide solutions to a whole array of problems. The primary one, of course, is finding new uses for a product. Baking soda, for example, isn't just for baking. It is useable as a refrigerator deodorizer, a cleanser, and as a teeth brightener.

In a related vein, a very humorous account of "20 better insults" for a character's quite long nose in the 1987 movie "Roxanne" catches the spirit of this technique, if not its actual functional focus. Steve Martin, as fire chief C. D Bales, has his long nose insulted by a bar patron. Turning the tables on his critic, he promptly chastises his antagonist for lack of creativity in the insult. Martin then reels off twenty super creative insults of his own nose. It's worth a look.

How many uses can you think of for a hammer? Name them.

1. _____   6. _____

2. _____   7. _____

3. _____   8. _____

4. _____   9. _____

5. _____   10. _____

If you want to find new uses for a product, you might be inspired by Velcro. Velcro is what you use to hold two pieces of cloth together, right? How many other uses could you think of for it? The chambers of the Jarvik-7 artifical heart are held together with Velcro for easy separation in case one side has to be replaced. Many things in the space shuttle are held together with Velcro, including parts of the rocket. Interior items, including astronauts, are held down by it. Velcro is used on blood pressure cuffs, to hold insulation in nuclear power plants, in machine gun turrets, on shoes in place of shoe strings, in automobiles to hold down batteries and spare tires, to hold together parts of an experimental car designed by Pontiac, to bind parts of airplane wings together, and to hold stamps to a letter carrier's mailbag. In fact, Velcro is a component of over 5000 patented products.[42]

Here's another example of multiple uses: Bruce DeWoolfson reasoned that if vending machines could spit out cans and bottles for a few coins they could just as easily spit out a few coins for empty cans and bottles, which could then be recycled. His firm places these "redeemer" machines in store throughout the states where recycling is mandated by law.[37]

You can use the same approach to find solutions to other problems. For instance, are you looking for a name for a product? Listing possible uses for it may suggest a good name.

49/23. THE NAPOLEON TECHNIQUE

Pretend that you are someone famous and try to solve the problem from that person's perspective.[44] Your assumed identity may give you new perspectives on a problem. For example, what would Isaac Newton do if he were confronted by your problem? General George Patton? Napoleon? Mother Theresa?

50/24. ORGANIZED RANDOM SEARCH

For many people a favorite way of coming up with new ideas is to pick a page of a dictionary at random and use the words on that page to generate ideas the way one uses a verbal checklist. You could use any book, even a catalog. Simply pick a page and look for words. Then use a two-dimensional matrix to compare the words on that page with an object or problem and/or its attributes. Sometimes you simply pick a word on that page and begin to make associations. This technique is often used by artists, writers, and others who depend on creativity for a livelihood. Managers at Current Inc., a greeting card company in Colorado Springs, picked the word "shrink." After a brainstorming session, they began Wee Greetings, a line of business and greeting cards that can be slipped into lunch boxes or shirt pockets.[45] This technique can also make use of pictures. For example, two telemarketing managers at Southern Bell leafed through fashion magazines for pictures that would trigger ideas for marketing campaigns.[46] Earlier, Google-storming was described as an Internet version of this technique.

51/25. PERSONAL ANALOGIES

An interesting type of analogy is the "personal analogy." In this approach you attempt to see yourself personally involved in the situation, perhaps through role playing. A major paper company found new uses for pulp and other tree parts and significantly raised profits when top managers role played the part of a tree going through the paper production process. In another instance, scientists working to develop a reflective window glass saw themselves as the molecules of the glass. They then asked themselves, "What has to happen to us to make us reflective?" On the basis of their answers, they developed the reflective glass used in many buildings today. In a third example, state officials in Ohio who wanted to write a comprehensive computer program to keep track of automobiles saw themselves as a car and asked, "What can happen to me?"

Finally, in a personal analogy/brainstorming session at Gillette, the managers saw themselves as human hairs. They imagined how a strand of hair would observe life. "I dread being washed every day." "I hate the blow-dryer." "I feel limp, lifeless." Some participants wanted a gentle shampoo to protect their damaged ends while others wanted a more aggressive one to really get the dirt out. Sandra Lawrence, Gillette's vice-president for new products, observed that "everyone had different sentiments, which made us think about how hair is different on different parts of the body." The result was Silkience, a shampoo that adapts itself to the different needs of different kinds of hair. Within one year, Silkience was one of the top ten shampoos in total sales.[47]

Envision yourself as the object or other problem that you are concerned about. See how your creativity is affected. Can you put yourself into your problem? Can you be your problem? What suggestions for solutions result?

SUMMARY OF STEPS

1. Become personally involved in the problem, perhaps through role playing or visualization.
2. Ask yourself what insights or potential solutions this involvement yields.

52/26.   PICTURE STIMULATION

The picture stimulation technique aims to provide ideas beyond those that might be obtained through basic brainstorming.[48] You view one or more pictures and then individually brainstorm ideas about your problem. Picture stimulation is somewhat similar to the excursion technique (see Chapter 5), except that the participants look at pictures instead of visualizing an excursion. In a group setting, discussion of the ideas suggested should not take place until the creative session is finished. Basic brainstorming rules should be followed. Using the Internet as a source of pictures works well in groups as well as individually. There are thousands of visual sources on the Internet. For example, Webshots.com allows you to download for free thousands of high quality photographs; Art.com offers reproductions of the works of many famous artists. Perusing their on-line catalog can provide many ideas; and most major art museums offer pictures of some or all of their works on their websites. Picture stimulation is excellent for getting to new ideas that wouldn't be spawned by your normal idea generation processes.

SUMMARY OF STEPS

1. Select pictures from various sources and present them for participants to view as projected images, slides, photos, etc. The pictures should show some action and not be too abstract.
2. Examine each picture and describe it to a recorder, who writes the description on a flip chart, white board, or other surface.
3. Use each line of the description to trigger new ideas, which are recorded separately.
4. Continue until all the pictures have been examined.

53/27. PRODUCT IMPROVEMENT CHECKLIST

Arthur B. VanGundy has developed a product improvement checklist (PICL) that functions in the same way as the other "relational word" techniques discussed in this chapter, for example, SCAMPER. VanGundy has included some terms that seem absurd at first but that can provide new thought patterns. A total of 526 words are included in his list. Here are some examples:

Try To:	Make It:
sketch it	soft
sew it	hard
hang it	vertical
deflate it	unbreakable
gasify it	triangular
Think Of:	**Take Away or Add:**
televisions	funnels
ants	grooves
the four seasons	alcohol
bacteria	Velcro
Sir Lancelot	power

VanGundy's PICL is quite effective. VanGundy has also developed a device that he calls the Circles of Creativity. It consists of several hundred words arranged on three concentric circles in categories such as "Try to...," "Make it ...," "Think about ...," "Imagine ...," "Add to or delete ..." Spinning the circles and using attached arrows results in several combinations of words that may suggest actions regarding an existing product or service. VanGundy has a web site on the Internet.

SUMMARY OF STEPS

1. Identify the product or service you wish to improve.
2. Take each of the words from the PICL and apply the verbs as directed to your product or service. Write down the results.
3. Decide which of the possible actions is most feasible.

54/28. RELATEDNESS

Coined by Donald Hambrick, the term "relatedness" refers to an exercise in which you list all businesses or products related to yours to help you think of new products for your company.[49] For example, suppose you own a radio station. Think of all the businesses even remotely related to yours: newspapers, magazines, TV, cable TV, broadcasting. Now think of businesses and products related to those: advertising, printing, publishing, satellite communication. What new products could your company generate in any of these businesses?

55/29. RELATIONAL WORDS

Relational word techniques are based on causing forced-relationships between words. Ideas then result from thinking about these relationships. Several such techniques exist. Among these are techniques that use verbs (SCAMPER which follows shortly), prepositions, and various types of other relational words. Also included are morphological analysis and the focused-object technique. Each of these techniques requires matching a set of descriptors against an object, a problem, an opportunity, a service, a process, another set of descriptors, or a set of titles such as product names.

Forced-relationship techniques can be used effectively by artists and writers and by marketers seeking to develop or name a new product. They can also be used to change something that already exists or when one is seeking a new and different idea rather than a solution to a specific problem. These techniques are not well suited to solving specific problems because they rely primarily on chance relationships, and the probability of such a relationship existing as a specific problem is remote. However, if your problem is to add creativity to an existing situation, these processes are excellent. Techniques 41/15 and 53/27 are also forced-relationship techniques.

Several relational word checklists exist. Two of them are provided on the following pages. With Crovitz's relational words and the prepositions, you are simply trying to create ideas that might lead to product or service improvements. A third checklist, SCAMPER, is presented later in the chapter. The explanation of SCAMPER provides specific examples of how you would apply these relational word techniques. With respect to Crovitz's relational words and VanGundy's prepositions, the words themselves are simply provided. When using these techniques, some of your results might not seem to make sense, but by looking at them closely you may be able to develop useful ideas.

SUMMARY OF STEPS

1. Identify the product or service to be altered, or the object to be changed.
2. Apply the words from the various checklists to this product, service or object, recording the results in the spaces provided on the forms.
3. Review the results to see if they suggest possible solutions.

Crovitz's Relational Words[50]

The words in this list are used to ask questions: What's about this problem? What's across from this problem? What comes after this problem? And so on. The purpose is to generate ideas. Once you have ideas, analyze them to see what solutions they suggest. Here is his list of relational words: about, across, after, against, among, and, as, at, because, before, _between, but, by, down, for, from, if, in, near, not, now, of, off, opposite, or, out, over, still, so, then, though, through, till, to, under, up, when, where, while, with.

VanGundy's Prepositions[51]

These words can be used in the same way as Crovitz's relational words and the verbs in SCAMPER (which follows shortly) above, along, amid, around, behind, below, beneath, beside, beyond, during, except, into, past, since, toward, throughout, upon, within, without.

56/30. REVERSAL-DEREVERSAL

The reversal-dereversal technique can provide insights into new solutions for a problem.[52] State the problem, using an action verb. Then take the antonym of that verb and solve the new problem created in this way. The solutions to that problem may give you ideas about solving the original problem. For example, "to improve the product" would reversal-dereversal as "to worsen" the product. If the product was a movie DVD, you could make it have only one medium—video or music but not both; you could reduce sound quality; you could add more commercials at the beginning of the video or insert them in them middle of the movie; you could eliminate all extra features; and so on. The opposites of these would normally help solve the original problem.

57/31. ROLLING IN THE GRASS OF IDEAS

This technique involves collecting as much material as you can about the problem at hand in an easily readable form— for example, summaries of related articles and books, the experiences of others, ideas that others have given you, and competitors' actions. You read through this material as rap lying on the floor of my office. One day I told students in my innovation class how I sometimes get ideas for articles, books, products, management problems, and other problems by reading through as much material as possible related to the problem at hand. I de-scribed how excited I get with all those ideas running through my head, and how insights seem to pop into my head as a result. The analogy to my dogs' behavior was a natu-ral: I am rolling in the grass of ideas.

SUMMARY OF STEPS

1. Collect information about your problem, making notes in an eas-ily readable form.
2. Read through all of your notes in one sitting so that all the ideas are in your brain at one time.
3. Allow natural incubation to occur and see what ideas de-velop.

58/32. SCAMPER

SCAMPER is an idea generating checklist based on action verbs which suggest changes to an existing product, service or process. This mnemonic was created by Bob Eberle from the verbal checklist originated by Alex Osborn, a pioneer in creativity technique development.[53] Osborn also originated brainstorming, a technique discussed earlier in this chapter.

Osborn's original verbal checklist was ordered as follows: put to other uses, adapt, modify, magnify, minify, substitute, rearrange, reverse, and combine. Eberle reordered these to make them easier to remember:

S = Substitute?
C = Combine?
A = Adapt?
M=Magnify? Modify?
P = Put to other uses?
E = Eliminate or minify?
R = Rearrange? Reverse?

The idea behind this verbal checklist is that an existing product, service, or process, whether one's own or a competitor's, can be improved if one applies a series of verbs and related questions to it and pursues the answers to see where they may lead. These verbs indicate possible ways to improve an existing product or service by making changes in it. In the case of Osborn's checklist, further alternatives may be suggested by the definitions and related statements accompanying each of the main verbs. For example, if the item under consideration is a laptop PC and you are pursuing the "minify" alternative, you might shrink the laptop into a "notebook" or "palm" computer or a high powered "PDA". Eberle kept all of Osborn's questions and added a few more. See Exhibit 4.1. Over the years thousands of organizations have used the verbal checklist and derivations such as SCAMPER to create or enhance thousands of products and services. One of my editors for a textbook I created using SCAMPER to change key book features found this checklist so useful that he distributed it to the sales force to obtain suggestions for subsequent editions.

To use SCAMPER:
1. Identify the item—the product, service, or process you want to improve.
2. Ask the SCAMPER questions about your item and see what new ideas emerge. Be sure to use the extensive expansion of these verbs provided in Exhibit 4.1.

EXHIBIT 4.1 SCAMPER VERBS AND RELATED QUESTIONS	
VERB	**RELATED ACTION QUESTIONS**
SUBSTITUTE?	Who else can be substituted? What else can be substituted? Can the rules be changed? Other ingredient? Other material? Other process or procedure? Other power? Other place? Other approach? What other part instead of this?
COMBINE?	What ideas can be combined? Can we combine purposes? How about an assortment? How about a blend, an alloy, an ensemble? Combine units? What other article could be merged with this? How could we package a combination? What can be combined to multiply possible uses? What materials could we combine? Combine appeals?
ADAPT?	What else is like this? What other idea does this suggest? Does the past offer a parallel? What could I copy? Whom could I emulate? What idea could I

	incorporate? What other process could be adapted? What else could be adapted? What different contexts can I put my concept in? What ideas outside my field can I incorporate?
MAGNIFY?	What can be magnified, made larger, or extended? What can be exaggerated? Overstated? What can be added? More time? Stronger? Higher? Longer? How about greater frequency? Extra features? What can add extra value? What can be duplicated? How could I carry it to a dramatic extreme?
MODIFY?	How can this be altered for the better? What can be modified? Is there a twist? Change meaning, color, motion, sound, odor, form, shape? Change name? Other changes? What changes can be made in the plans? In the process? In marketing? What other form could this take? What other package? Can the package be combined with the form?
PUT TO OTHER USES?	What else can this be used for? Are there new ways to use as is? Other uses if modified? What else could be made from this? Other extensions? Other markets?
ELIMINATE OR MINIFY?	What if this were smaller? What should I omit? Should I divide it? Split it up? Separate it into different parts? Understate? Streamline? Make miniature? Condense? Compact? Subtract? Delete? Can the rules be eliminated? What's not necessary? What would a process flow chart reveal?

REARRANGE?	What other arrangement might be better? Interchange components? Other pattern? Other layout? Other sequence? Change the order? Transpose cause and effect? Change pace? Change schedule?
REVERSE?	Can I transpose positive and negative? What are the opposites? What are the negatives? Should I turn it around? Up instead of down? Down instead of up? Consider it backwards? Reverse roles? Do the unexpected?

Source: Created from text in Michael Michalko, *Thinkertoys* (Berkeley, California: Ten Speed Press, 1991), pp. 71–108.

Exhibit 4.2 is an example of SCAMPER used in a service industry—the hotel industry. Consider the traditional check-out procedure in a hotel. How can SCAMPER help us generate ideas for improving the process?

EXHIBIT 4.2 A SCAMPER EXAMPLE

ITEM: Traditional Check-out Procedure	
SUBSTITUTE	Check-out by phone, by in-house television channel, by mail; allow check-out at breakfast...
COMBINE	Combine check-out payment with check-in; offer breakfast food at check-out location; combine with services for ground transportation; combine with morning work-out at hotel exercise facility...
ADAPT	Adapt to the location of the guest; accept more credit cards; adapt to the times that guests want to check-out...
MAGNIFY	Increase the number of people at the check-out desk; make a big production out of check-out so that the guest enjoys it—have trumpets and encourage employees to weep as the guest leaves; have a very large

	person at the check-out desk so that the guest will be afraid to complain...
MODIFY or MINIFY	Have all forms and bills prepared before the guest comes to check out so that the least amount of time is required; cut some steps out of the current process; computerize to increase speed...
PUT TO OTHER USES	While the guests are waiting to check out, interview them about their stay and how the hotel could be improved; use check-out time as an opportunity to advertise specials that the hotel will be offering in the future; ask the guests if they wouldn't mind washing some windows for you while waiting to check-out...
ELIMINATE	No check-out—the guest leaves a credit card or a large deposit with you upon arrival so that you don't have to collect money upon departure. Or, do not allow any guests to leave the hotel once they come in—this will significantly increase occupancy...
REARRANGE	Rearrange the check-out area; rearrange the procedure for check-out...
REVERSE	Come to the guest's room and allow them to check out there; have guests check out when they arrive and check in when they depart (we don't know, you figure it out)...

Source: Florence Berger and Dennis H. Ferguson, *Innovation: Creativity Techniques for Hospitality Managers* (New York: John Wiley & Sons, Inc., 1990), pp. 25–26.

SUMMARY OF STEPS

1. Identify the product or service to be modified.
2. Apply each of the verbs on the checklist to suggest changes in the product or service writing the changes in the blank spaces on the form provided.
3. Make sure you use each of the action questions for the listed verbs in identifying possible changes.
4. Review your changes to determine which ones meet your criteria.

Here are some additional verbs that might be used beyond what you have found in SCAMPER. You would use them in the same way, forcing them against your product, service, process, or object to be changed.

Verbal Relational-Word Checklist:[54]

Multiply, divide, eliminate, subdue, invert, separate, transpose, unify, dissect, distort, rotate, flatten, squeeze, complement, submerge, freeze, soften, fluff-up, by-pass, add, subtract, widen, repeat, thicken, stretch, extrude, help, protect, segregate, integrate, symbolize, abstract, etc. (*Source*: unknown)

59/33 7 x 7 TECHNIQUE

Another way to improve the utilization of new ideas is the 7 x 7 technique, a series of exercises designed to process, organize and evaluate idea slips that have been mounted on a racking board in seven rows and seven columns (or more, if needed).[55] Carl Gregory, who developed this technique, suggests that the following steps can help you make sense of all your ideas. You might use suggestions for this technique with a similar process, storyboarding (see Chapter 5):

1. Combine similar ideas.
2. Exclude irrelevant data.
3. Modify ideas to reflect insights gained in the first two steps.
4. Defer extraneous data for future reference.
5. Review past exercises to identify possibilities for alteration or refinement.
6. Classify dissimilar groupings into separate columns.
7. Rank items in each column.
8. Generalize each column using its main idea as a heading or title.
9. Rank the columns from left to right on the racking board according to their importance or utility.

Brief explanations of these steps follow.

Combine

When you have at least two racking boards filled with idea slips or when your pile of ideas is exhausted, read each idea bit carefully. Discard any redundant information and combine similar ideas. Give each grouping of related ideas a title.

Exclude

Exclude all things that are not related to the objective of the exercise or are too "far out" for present consideration. Put the excluded ideas into another pile for later use.

Modify

Where necessary, write new statements of ideas that have been modified as a result of the first two steps.

Defer

Put into a separate category any item that is not particularly timely but may be useful later. Defer is similar to exclude except the criteria are different.

Feedback

Review the ideas that have been combined, eliminated, modified, or deferred to seek new insights.

Classify by Dissimilar Columns

Establish a column for each group of related ideas. Despite the name of the technique, seven is not a magic number: eight, nine, ten, or more columns may be necessary.

Rank Ideas in Each Column

When you have sorted all the ideas into columns, rank each idea card on the basis of the usefulness or importance of the idea relative to the objective.

Generalize Columns

It is often advantageous to provide a title for each column, as in storyboarding. You could probably put those which are similar under the same column heading. Alternatively, the highest-ranking idea in each column could serve as the heading.

Rank Columns

Place the best, most important, timeliest, or most critical ideas in the left-hand column, the second-most important in the next column to the right, and so on.

There are many variations on the 7 x 7 technique. Like storyboarding, it can be used in group sessions.

SUMMARY OF STEPS
1. Place idea slips on a 7 x 7 racking board.
2. Combine, exclude, modify, defer, feedback, classify, and rank ideas within columns; generalize the columns; and then rank the columns.
3. Evaluate the results.

60/34. SLEEPING/DREAMING ON IT

One of the easiest ways to generate alternatives is to think rationally, very hard, and very long about a problem just before going to sleep. Put it out of your mind and then go to sleep. When you wake up in the morning, the odds are that you will have come up with an interesting alternative or series of alternatives for solving the problem. The reason this technique works so well is that your subconscious continues to work on the problem while you are asleep.[56]

Thomas Edison often used brief periods of sleep to develop ideas. He would sit in a chair and holding pebbles in his hands allow himself to fall asleep while thinking about a problem. As he fell asleep, the pebbles would fall from his hands into tin plates on the floor. This, he claimed, helped him come up with new ideas by taking advantage of his subconscious efforts to solve problems in a state of near-sleep.[57]

Solutions to complex problems often appear in dreams. The concept of the benzene molecule came to German chemist Friedrick August Kelkule in a dream. He saw a snake biting its own tail and realized that the benzene molecule was a closed loop, not an open one. Noted writer Robert Louis Stevenson, who often used his subconscious to develop story ideas, reports that the characters of Dr. Jekyll and Mr. Hyde came to him in a dream.[58]

SUMMARY OF STEPS

1. Think long and hard about your problem just before going to sleep and as you begin to drift off.
2. If you awake during the night with a solution or other ideas, write them down on notecards that you have left on the nightstand next to your bed.
3. When you awake in the morning, think about your thoughts and dreams and see if they suggest solutions to your problem. Write the possible solutions on notecards.

61/35. TRIZ

In 1948, Genrich Altshuller, a 22 year-old lieutenant in the Caspian Sea Military Navy sent a letter to Comrade Stalin describing the Soviet Union's approach to technology as chaotic and dysfunctional. In his letter he wrote Stalin that he had developed a systematic approach which he wanted to share with the fatherland. A year later, Soviet officials invited him to Tbiisi, Georgia, USSR, to further discuss his system. Upon his arrival, he was arrested and sentenced to 25 years in the Gulag. Shortly after Stalin's death in 1953, Altshuller was released and began to refine and interest others in his system which has become known as TRIZ.

TRIZ (pronounced *trees*) is partly a problem defining system but also a powerful solution generating system. Altshuller's system is based on extensive research of over 200,000 patents (eventually a 1,500,000 were examined). Altshuller evaluated approximately only 40,000 of these 200,000 patented solutions as being really inventive, the rest he perceived as being the results of straight forward improvements. He described inventive problems as ones in which a solution might lead to another problem such as the one involved when increasing the strength of a metal plate typically increases its weight. It was to solve inventive problems that his system was developed.

Altshuller subsequently proposed that every technical problem that required real creativity and innovation involved conflicts at its core—for example, dry something, but consume less energy; or make a powerful engine but make it lighter; or build a higher capacity hard drive but make it smaller. After examining these 200,000 plus patents, he sorted the sources of conflict into 39 categories, for example, strength, stability, brightness, volume, temperature, and so on. He also found 40 common solution paths that had led to creative solutions, what are known as the "40 principles," for example, segmentation, asymmetry, and pneumatic or hydraulic construction.

His work is so impactful because he not only found out that the same problems were being solved over and over again, he also found solutions for most of these "inventive problems." He realized that if only others had known of the common solution paths, they would literally not have had to invent the wheel again. To enable his system to be readily useable, he created a matrix of conflicts and related solutions. The 39 causes of conflicts are labeled as "feature to be improved" on one axis and "undesired result" on the other axis. At the intersection of each of these pairs Altshuller has provided solutions to the conflicting requirements of the two characteristics—the 40 principles. Typically more than one principle is listed when Altshuller provides solutions at the intersections on the matrix, but many cases, Altshuller does not provide any recommendations.

It has taken some time for TRIZ to become known in the US. Altshuller's work had to be translated and then made known outside the USSR. But in recent years it has begun to have a substantial impact on creative problem solving in several large US corporations such as Ford Motor Company, Dow Chemical, and HP/Compaq. What is important to recognize is that the 39 causes of conflict and the 40 principles are models and finding the analogous solution is not always easy. Interpretation and creativity are necessary and a certain level of skill is required, but acquiring a sufficient level of these skills can be accomplished in a day or so.[59]

62/36. THE TWO-WORDS TECHNIQUE

The meaning you give to certain words can block your ability to solve a problem. With the two-words technique you pick the two words or phrases from your problem statement that indicate its essence. The problem statement always includes a subject (or objective) and an action verb. Normally you focus on these in the two-words technique.[60]

For example, suppose that the problem statement is "Reduce absenteeism." You have been unable to generate many new ideas about how to solve the problem. You might list the following alternate words:

reduce	absenteeism
diminish	out
decrease	away
shorten	not in
curtail	not present
lessen	lacking
contract	missing

Then you might try combining these words in various ways. The following ideas could result:

1. Design an absenteeism program in which employees are given a certain number of days per year for "no excuse needed" absences (diminish/not in).

2. Survey employees to find what might be lacking in the workplace to cause them to be absent (decrease/lacking).

3. Lower the penalty for unauthorized absences if the absence was for less than a day (shorten/out).

4. Allow employees to be absent a specified number of days during a given quarter if they make up for them during the next quarter (curtail/away).

5. Offer employees the opportunity to benefit from self- or professional-development programs on the job. This might increase their motivation and decrease the number of absences (less/lacking)."

This is an excellent technique for overcoming definitional problems, but it can also be used to generate new ideas even if you aren't having problems with the definitions of terms.

SUMMARY OF STEPS

1. Select two key words or phrases (usually the action verb and the objective) from the problem statement.
2. List alternate words for each word or phrase (a thesaurus or dictionary may be helpful).
3. Select the first word from the first list and combine it with the first word from the second list.
4. Examine this combination and see if it suggests any ideas. If so, write them down.
5. Combine the first word from the first list with the second word from the second list, etc.
6. Continue combining words from the two lists and writing down ideas until you have examined all possible combinations.

63/37. VISUALIZATION

Visualization of a problem and its potential solutions is a good way to generate alternatives. The mind seems to react even more creatively to pictures than to words. Visualization seems to evoke new insights, which can lead to new solutions. This process can be used in conjunction with other processes.[61] Simply close your eyes and visualize the problem. What do you see? Expand on what you see. Seek more detail. What do your visions suggest? What solutions can you see?

64/38 WHAT IF...?

Ask yourself "What if something happens, what would the consequences be?" For example, what if you sold a million units of your product next year? What consequences would occur? Who would be affected? What actions should you take? Or if your sales dropped by 10 percent, how would your firm be affected? What should you do?

This technique can be a powerful tool. Successful strategic management often depends on the ability to ask "What if?" questions and then generate a list of consequences and strategic responses. Firms often use "What if?" scenarios to formulate strategic plans and strategic contingency plans. Strategic "What ifs?" can be enhanced greatly in terms of measuring impacts with the use of various software packages, for example, spreadsheets.

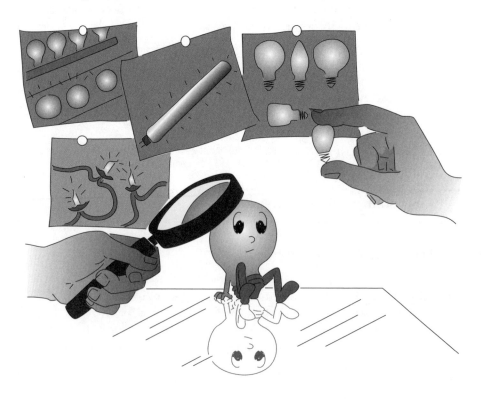

"What if?" can also be used at and have a major impact on every level of a company. For example, when General Electric Company CEO Jeffrey Immelt decided that the strategic thrusts of the company needed to be more focused on innovation and marketing, he realized that it would be necessary to change the engineering, process and financial controls oriented GE culture. Immelt appointed Beth Comstock as the company's first ever chief marketing officer and charged her with achieving this cultural change. "Creativity is still a word we're wrestling with," Comstock concedes. "It seems a bit undisciplined, a bit chaotic for a place like GE." She indicates that for GE, a more comfortable term is "imaginative problem-solving"—encouraging people to think "what if?"—yet always with the aim of driving growth. Comstock has instituted a number of training and development programs to help instill a culture more receptive to and promoting of innovation. "We have a long way to go," she says. It isn't that easy to change 300,000 people. But as *Business Week* writer Diane Brady notes, "But for GE, there's no turning back."[62]

CREATIVITY AND INNOVATION ARE NOT EASY

Chapter 1 discussed the criticality of creativity and innovation to corporate growth and success; and that chapter also alluded to the difficulties involved in sustaining both of these. While you still have numerous creativity techniques to review, now that you have examined a large number of them, it is appropriate to revisit these issues again in order to put creativity techniques into perspective. Creative Edge in Action 4.2 examines the difficulties Sony faces in staying competitive because it has not remained innovative, and it has also made some bad choices about where to focus its creativity and innovation efforts.

SONY'S COMPETITIVE CHALLENGES

When Britisher Howard Stringer succeeded Nobuyuki Idei as CEO of Sony in June of 2005, he inherited, in one word, a "mess." For starters, Sony long heralded as an innovative juggernaut, had lost its touch. It was consistently being beaten in the market place by more nimble and more innovative companies. For example, Apple caught Sony flat-footed with the iPod, Samsung (among others) beat Sony to the punch with successful flat panel TV screens, and Sony's Cyber Shot camera line while stylish lacked many of the features that consumers wanted such as longer battery life and a larger LCD screen. Sony's business model had called for first to market products such as Walkman and superior technology products such as Triniton TVs for which Sony was then able to garner a premium price. But now lacking both first to market and technology superiority, the Sony brand could no longer demand higher prices. And in some of their markets, such as PCs, Sony lost substantial market share because that industry was commoditizing and Sony was still seeking a premium for a what had become just another product. Sony also suffered from a relatively high cost structure compared to most of its competitors. Without much differentiation and with relatively high cost, Sony struggled to make a profit in 2005.

What are some of the causes of Sony's apparent loss of innovation capacity? First, Sony operates with business units that have virtual total autonomy. Competition and lack of cooperation among these units has been deadly in a time of technological integration. In addition, Sony is very bureaucratic. The decision process is slow in a time when speed to market is everything. Third, Sony is mired in businesses that use antiquated technologies such as cathode-ray tube TVs and analog based mini-disc Walkman audio players. The world has moved on to plasma screens and audio systems that feature hard disc drives and memory cards thus leaving Sony behind. Furthermore, despite his success in turning around Sony's US based entertainment division, as the first non-Japanese to head Sony, Stringer was an outsider. He did not speak Japanese and in addition, internal politics had played an important role in Idei's inability to make much needed changes in Sony. Thus Stringer had to manage that issue as well.

Sony is a good example of how companies can choose the wrong areas to innovate in, or not to innovate in. So no matter how good they may be fundamentally at innovation, they are using those skills incorrectly. And Sony also is a good example of how poor management and politics can lead to the wrong structures as well as the wrong product choices. And these in turn lead to slow speed to market and a lack of management innovation.

Product choices, product development, product design, process design and management innovation are the kinds of innovation which can be driven by the creativity techniques discussed in this book. Of course the underlying scientific skills must be there for product research and development, but there is much to do beyond the basic science and this is where creativity techniques are so valuable.

Source: Michiyo Nakamoto, "Screen Test: Stringer's Strategy Will Signal to what Extent Sony Can Stay in the Game." *Financial Times* (September 21, 2005), p. 13 provides the information on Sony. The closing materials represent the considered opinions of Jim Higgins.

TWO FINAL NOTES

1. There are thirty-eight processes discussed in this chapter. Some you will like, some you won't, but try as many of them as you can. Then use the ones you feel most comfortable with, but revisit the rest of these processes occasionally to make sure you aren't overlooking one that might be of value in your particular situation.

2. You have ideas all the time. They come to you in the shower, while sleeping, while driving. Keep a notebook or 3 x 5 cards handy to write your ideas on. You can examine them later. *Once forgotten, an idea may be lost forever. So write it down! Now!*

Table 4.3

A QUICK GUIDE TO MY FAVORITE TECHNIQUES FOR GENERATING ALTERNATIVES*

Technique	Best Use
SCAMPER/Product Improvement Checklist	For redesigning existing products and services
Mind Mapping	To let ideas flow freely; for designing outlines; for collecting thoughts about an issue
Association/ Free Association	When you need lots of ideas quickly and a way to relate them to problems; when normal processes haven't provided many ideas
Google Storming; Picture Stimulation (Related)	Relate them to problems; when normal processes haven't provided many ideas.
Rolling in the Grass of Ideas	For gaining new insights, combining ideas, and solving complex problems about which much is known

Technique	Best Use
Brainstorming	For simple problems when solutions are needed quickly
Lotus Blossom	To generate lots of ideas quickly to size up a problem; excellent for developing future scenarios
Storyboarding	For understanding issues involved in complex problems, and for solving complex problems
Excursion	When problem is difficult to solve, when it has been hard to generate ideas using other techniques
Nominal Group Technique	Especially useful when you want to keep one person from dominating the choice among alternatives
Morphological Analysis	For generating lots of ideas quickly about product or service improvements

**All except the nominal group technique can be used individually as well as in a group.

124

REFERENCES

[1] Kamal S. Birdi, "No Idea? Evaluating the Effectiveness of Creativity Training," *Journal of European Industrial Training* (Issue 2/3, 2005), pp. 102-111 reviews one related study; Ginamarie Scott, Lyle E. Leritz, and Michael D. Mumford, "The Effectiveness of Creativity Training: A Quantitative Review," *Creativity Research Journal* (Issue 4, 2004), pp. 361-380 reviews several related studies.

[2] Bruce Nussbaum, "Get Creative," *Business Week* (August 1, 2005), pp. 60-68; "Special Report—The Innovation Economy," *Business Week* (October 11, 2004), throughout. Also see endnote 19 for Chapter 1 for a sizeable list of related studies.

[3] David Kohn, "The Darwinian Police Sketch with Crime-Fighting Software Inspired by Evolution, A Picture Is Worth a Thousand...other Pictures," *Popular Science* (July 2005), p. 32.

[4] Charles W. Petit, "Touched by Nature: Putting Evolution to Work on the Assembly Line," *U.S. News & World Report* (July 27, 1998), pp. 43-46.

[5] Peter Rodelsky, "The Man Who Mastered Motion," *Science* (May 1986), pp. 53, 54.

[6] Magaly Olivero, "Get Crazy! How to Have a Breakthrough Idea," *Working Woman* (September 1990), p. 198.

[7] Brian Burlacoff and Mark Coutts, "Conceptual Selling: Simple Ideas to Ignite your Selling," *National Underwriter* (July 4-July 11, 2005), pp. 14-16; Robert W. Boozer, David C. Wyld, and James Grant, "Using Metaphor to Create More Effective Sales Messages," *Journal of Services Marketing* (Summer 1990), pp. 63-71.

[8] Ikujiro Nonaka, "The Knowledge-Creating Company," *Harvard Business Review* (November-December 1991), p. 100.

[9] Kristi Arrellano, "Gap Upgrades Design of Colorado Stores to Cater to Older, Upscale Customer," *Knight Ridder Tribune Business News* (April 22, 2005), p. 1.

[10] Thomas M. Burton, "By Learning from Failures, Lily Keeps Drug Pipeline Full," *Wall Street Journal* (April 21, 2004), pp. A1, A12.

[11] Source unknown.

[12] Robert Spitzer, "Collective Creativity," *Executive Excellence* (August 2000), p. 14; Tristram Korten, "The Creative Spark," *Design News* (February 12, 1990), p. 136.

[13] Mark Golin, "How to Brainstorm by Yourself ... and Triple the Results," *Young Executive* (Spring 1992), p. 75.

[14] Bryan W. Mattimore, "Breakthroughs: Creatively Destroying the Barriers to Business Innovation," *Success* (November 1988), p. 46.

[15] Arthur B. VanGundy, *Creative Problem Solving* (New York: Quorum Books, 1987), pp. 123-124.

[16] Charles S. Whiting, "Operational Techniques of Creative Thinking," *Advanced Management* (October 1955), p. 26.

[17] Bruce Nussbaum, "The Power of Design," *Business Week* (May 17, 2004), pp. 86-94.

[18] Dan Koberg and Jim Bagnall, *Universal Traveler* (Los Altos, CA: William Kaufman, Inc., 1974), p. 50.

[19] Michael Michalko, *Thinkertoys: A Handbook of Business Creativity for the 1990s* (Berkeley, California: 1991), pp. 181-185.

[20] Joseph M. Winski, "Big Idea in a Box," *Advertising Age* (March 25, 1991), p. 31; E. W. Brody, "Software Review: Idea Fisher 3.0," *Public Relations Review* (Winter 1990), pp. 67-68.

[21] Winski, op. cit.; Bryan W. Mattimore, "Mind Blasters: Software to Shatter Brain Block," *Success* (June 1990), pp. 46, 47.

[22] Jenny C. McCune, "Creativity Catalysts," *Success* (July-August 1992), p. 50.

[23] Brian Mattimore, "The Amazing Invention Machine," *Success* (October 1993), p. 34.

[24] Teresa Amabile, "Creativity Under the Gun," *Harvard Business Review* (August 2002), pp. 62-70.

[25] Berkeley Rice, "Imagination to Go," *Psychology Today* (May 1984), p. 48.

[26] "Want to Design a Robot? Try Watching a Bug," *Business Week* (1986); Magaly Olivero, op. cit., p. 148.

[27] James Braham, "Creativity: Eureka!" *Machine Design* (February 6, 1992), p. 37.

[28] Michael Michalko, op. cit., pp. 126-131.

[29] Michael E. Porter, *Competitive Advantage* (New York: Free Press, 1985), pp. 131-151.

[30] Charles S. Whiting, op. cit., p. 29.

[31] Carl E. Gregory, *The Management of Intelligence* (New York: McGraw-Hill, 1962), pp. 45-51.

[32] Dan Koberg and Jim Bagnall, op. cit., p. 27.

[33] Tony Buzan, *The Mind Map Book* (London: BBC Worldwide, 2003); Tony Buzan, "Mind mapping," *Success* (April 1997), p. 30; Tony Buzan, *Use Both Sides of Your Brain*, (New York: E. P. Dutton, Inc., 1983).

[34] Joyce Wycoff, *Mind Mapping*, (Berkley Publishing Group: 1991).

[35] Daren A. Brown and Nancy Lee Hyer, "Whole-Brain Thinking for Project Management," *Business Horizons* (May-June 2002), pp. 47-53.

[36] Lars Torsten Eriksson and Amie M. Hauer, "Mind Map Marketing: A Creative Approach in Developing Marketing Skills," *Journal of Marketing Education* ('August 2004), pp. 174-199.

[37] Jill Neimark, "Mind Mapping," *Success* (June 1986), pp. 52–57.

[38] Anthony J. Mento, Raymond M. Jones, and Walter Dimdorfer, "A Change Management Process: Grounded in Both Theory and Practice," *Journal of Change Management* (Issue 1, 2002), pp. 45-59.

[39] James Braham, op. cit., p. 33.

[40] Jill Neimark, op. cit.

[41] Andi Esposito, "Music Makes Their World Go Round: A Creative Outlet for Many Engineers," *Telegram and Gazette* (December 17, 2000), p. E. 1.; Anne H. Rosenfeld, "Music, The Beautiful Disturber," *Psychology Today* (December 1985), pp. 48–56; 71.

[42] Judith Stone, "Velcro: The Final Frontier," *Discover* (May 1988), pp. 82-84.

[43] About the Company, www.Envipco.com/envipco.asp, September 2, 2005; "Inside Track: Finding Riches in Garbage," *Success* (May 1987), p. 30.

[44] Bryan W. Mattimore, "Breakthroughs: Creatively Destroying the Barriers to Business Innovation," *Success* (November 1988), p. 48.

[45] Emily T. Smith, "Are You Creative?" *Business Week* (September 30, 1985), p. 48.

[46] Author's conversation with these two attendees at one of my seminars.

[47] Magaly Olivero, op. cit., p. 145.

[48] Arthur B. VanGundy, *Creative Problem Solving*, op. cit., pp. 136-137.

[49] "Buzzword of the Month," *Success* (November 1985), p. 20.

[50] H.F. Crovitz, *Galton's Walk* (New York: Harper & Row, 1970).

[51] Arthur B. VanGundy, *Techniques of Structured Problem Solving* (New York: Van Norstrand Reinhold, 1988), p. 105.

[52] Edward Glassman, "Creative Problem Solving," *Supervisory Management* (March 1989), pp. 14-18.

[53] Robert Eberle, *SCAMPER: Games for Imagination Development* (Buffalo, New York: D.O.K. Press, 1972); Alex F. Osborn, *Applied Imagination* (New York: Charles Scribner's & Sons, 1953).

[54] Source unknown.

[55] Carl E. Gregory, op. cit., pp. 45-51.

[56] Sue Palmer, "While They Are Sleeping..." *The Time Educational Supplement* (March 18, 2005), p. 24; Anahad O'Connor, "Really?" *The New York Times* (November 9, 2004), p. F.6; Ullrich Wagner, Steffen Gais, Hilde Haider, Rolf Verleger and Jan Born, "Sleep Inspires Insight," *Nature* (January 22, 2004), p. 352; Pierre Maquet and Perrine Ruby, "Insight and the Sleep Committee," *Nature* (January 22, 2004), p. 304; Deirdre Barrett, *The Committee of Sleep* (New York: Crown, 2001) provides a thorough discussion and numerous anecdotes related to sleep and how it enables creativity.

[57] From a lecture given in the guided tour of Edison's winter home in Ft. Myers, Florida, May 17, 1987.

[58] Robert Wayne Johnston, "Using Dreams for Creative Problem Solving," *Personnel* (November 1987), pp. 58–63; Edward Ziegler, "Dreams: The Genie Within," *Reader's Digest* (September 1985), pp. 77–81.

[59] Glenn Mazur, "Theory of Inventive Problem Solving," found at www.mazur.net/triz on September 2, 2005; Andy Raskin, "A Higher Plane of Problem-Solving," *Business 2.0* (June 2003), pp. 54-56.

[60] Arthur B. VanGundy, *Creative Problem Solving*, op. cit., pp. 118-120.

[61] Lea Hall, "Can You Picture That?" *Training & Development Journal* (September 1990), pp. 79-81.

[62] Diane Brady, "The Transformer: Beth Comstock," *Business Week* (August 1, 2005), p. 77.

CHAPTER

4

127

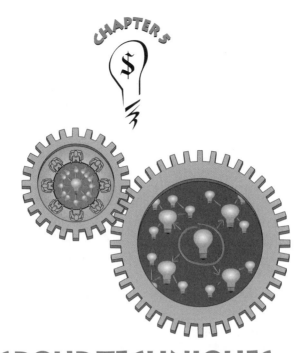

GROUP TECHNIQUES
FOR
GENERATING ALTERNATIVES

No longer does innovation reside solely in isolated research labs and ivory towers. In a globally integrated economy, with open source technologies and industry standards increasingly coming to play, innovation is a team sport.

Samuel Palmisano, CEO of IBM

IBM's CEO Samuel Palmisano isn't just talking about internal teams in this chapter's opening quote. He's also talking about teams formed across companies and often formed around the globe as alliances and other such collaborative efforts are increasingly vital to global success. This is just one of many reasons that in order to elicit the best ideas from their employees, companies such as IBM, Georgia-Pacific, W.R. Grace, Sun Life Financial, and Chevron have turned to online brainstorming. These companies report that their online sessions have not only led to significant cost savings, but also to the development of new products and new uses for old products. Mark Turrell,

CEO of Boston based innovation consulting and software firm Imaginatik, observes that, "In the global economy American isn't the low cost producer, so you need great brainpower. Where else is your value added?"[1]

Exactly! Today, companies must add significant value in order to survive and prosper, and in a knowledge based economy much of that value added is going to come from employee ideas. "According to a study by PriceWaterhouseCoopers, almost half (45%) of lucrative ideas—whether break-through products or services, new uses for old ones, or ways to cut costs—come from employees. (Customers, suppliers, and competitors contribute the other half.)"[2] And since much of today's work is performed in groups, many of today's management approaches focus on groups of employees such as autonomous work teams and project teams, or on virtual teams which do not actually physically meet but rather meet online. Moreover, in recent years teams have been one of the primary mechanisms used to improve quality, productivity, and innovation, for example through work group based quality management programs or through new product or process design, development, and improvement teams.

Since both research and experience indicate that groups usually provide better solutions than individuals, it makes sense to understand and be able to use group-based techniques for generating creative alternatives. And if you, as a manager or small-group/team leader or member want your team to be more effective, you will want to train the members of your group in the processes that make teams more successful in generating creative alternatives. Online brain-storming is just one of many techniques discussed in this chapter.

This chapter first discusses the advantages and disadvantages of group based decision making and then reviews in some detail the major group-based techniques for generating alternatives, for example, brainstorming, excursion, group decision support systems (including electronic brainstorming), lotus blossom, morphological analysis, nominal-group, storyboarding, and synectics. Several other group processes are discussed briefly. At the end of this chapter are several suggestions for maximizing the use of group techniques.

There are two primary types of groups: interactive and non-interactive. In interactive groups the participants meet face-to-face; in non-interactive groups, participants do not meet face-to-face. Except for the Delphi technique, the processes discussed in this chapter involve interactive groups. Online groups are somewhat of an anomaly. They do not meet face to face, but they may be interactive.

ADVANTAGES AND DISADVANTAGES OF GROUP DECISION MAKING

Groups offer six advantages over individual decision making and problem solving:
1. The group can usually provide a better solution to a problem than can an individual. Collectively the members of a group have more knowledge than an individual. Interactive groups not only combine this knowledge but create a knowledge base greater than the sum of its parts as individuals build on each other's inputs.
2. Those who will be affected by a decision or must implement it accept it more readily if they have a say in making it.
3. Group participation leads to a better understanding of the decision.
4. Groups help ensure a broader search effort.
5. The propensity to take risks is balanced. Individuals who are highly likely to take risks often fail. Groups moderate this tendency. Conversely, groups encourage the risk avoider to take more risks.
6. There is usually a better collective judgment.

On the other hand, there are some liabilities to employing group decision making and problem solving:

1. In interactive groups there is pressure to conform. Sometimes these groups become susceptible to what is known as "group think," in which people begin to think

alike and not tolerate new ideas or ideas contrary to those of the group.

2. One individual may dominate the interactive group so that his or her opinions prevail over those of the group. Nominal groups, where secret ballots and time constraints on idea descriptions are used, are designed to overcome this problem.

3. Groups typically require more time to come to decisions than individuals do.

4. Although groups usually make better decisions than the average individual, they seldom make better ones than the superior individual. In fact, superior performance by a group may result from the efforts of one superior group member.

5. Spending an excessive amount of time arriving at a consensus may negate the advantages of a good decision.

6. Groups sometimes make riskier decisions than they should. This propensity of groups is known as the risky shift.

When you weigh the pros and cons, the advantages win out. But when you are using groups to generate creative solutions don't forget their limitations.

USING CREATIVITY TECHNIQUES WITH SMALL GROUPS

By now you may be wondering how groups might use creativity techniques. Creative Edge in Action 5.1 describes the successful experience of one company which used various creativity techniques with small groups during a company retreat focused on developing new product ideas. Virtually any problem can be attacked by small groups using creativity techniques.

BRAINSTORMING FOR NEW PRODUCTS

When American Financial Products, Inc. experienced a plateau in its earnings for the first time in its 20 year history, its senior managers recognized the need to significantly increase the number of new products in its product pipeline. Maria Alverez, recently appointed vice-president for product design and development, was tasked with increasing the number of successful products in the pipeline by at least two in the next six months, and ten in the next year and a half. The company kept a list of products that had been "thought about," what some companies call a parking lot, and that list numbered about 200. Maria knew from experience at her most recent position with another company that sometimes some of these product ideas can be resurrected. What often occurs is that the reasons for objections to the products may have gone away, or the objectors may have moved on. But she also knew that most of these ideas wouldn't stand a chance of passing the various hurdles that they would face, both administrative and political.

So seizing the initiative as was expected of her, she immediately set about to gather together the top 50 "leading edge thinkers" in this company of some 2000 employees for two, one day "brainstorming" sessions for identifying new product ideas. She recognized the need to have forward looking sales people, product managers, IT people (Information Technology was an important part of several product offerings), and key members of the product design and development team as part of this group of 50. She arranged for a facilitator familiar with creativity techniques to lead the groups since she wanted to participate in the sessions herself. Together she and the facilitator formulated a plan for running the sessions. Many factors were considered. As always happens, availability of personnel dictated to some extent the members who would attend one day versus the other.

Because they wanted to keep people fresh and the ideas flowing, more than one creativity technique was used. Four techniques—SCAMPER, mind mapping, storyboarding, and excursion were all used for the sessions. Groups of five or six spent approximately an hour and a half first learning a technique, then brainstorming ideas, and then identifying their top five ideas. Four or five different key areas, depending on time availability were addressed each day. In the end some 350 ideas were generated, and each day the top ten for that day were identified by a simple show of hands. Then the real work began of first taking these ideas, running them through a series of idea evaluation hurdles provided by a strategic management consulting group, and then taking the few best and selling them to

CREATIVE EDGE IN ACTION 5.1

133

management. When reflecting on the two day retreat, Maria felt it had been an unqualified success.

Source: Information obtained from the facilitator James Higgins.

GROUP PROCESSES FOR GENERATING CREATIVE ALTERNATIVES

The remainder of this chapter examines the various group processes for generating alternatives. Don't overlook any of them, since they may all help you in one way or another. I try to use them all occasionally, although, my favorites are these four:

65/1.   Brainstorming
73/9.   Excursion
81/17. Lotus blossom
93/29. Storyboarding

See Table 4.4 for a quick guide to these processes.

65/1.   BRAINSTORMING

Brainstorming is one of the most effective, and probably the most widely used, of the group processes[3] It was created over sixty years ago by Alex Osborn of the advertising firm of Batten, Barton, Durstine and Osborn to increase the quantity and quality of advertising ideas.[4] The process became known as brainstorming because the participants' brains were used to "storm" a problem. Alternative solutions are offered verbally by group members in spontaneous fashion as they think of them. The leader acknowledges each contribution, which is recorded on a board for all to see. Wild and crazy ideas are encouraged. Users seek quantity, not quality, at first. In the initial session there is no discussion or criticism. The ideas are evaluated at later meetings of the same group.

Brainstorming Is a Critical Ingredient in Other Techniques: Brainstorming is not only a major creativity technique in its own right, but what makes being able to use it successfully so critical is that many other techniques rely on the brainstorming process and its rules as the underlying process in those techniques. For example storyboarding, an often used group technique which is especially good for solving complex problems, is essentially structured brainstorming with a column and rows format. Much the same could be said for mind mapping and SCAMPER when they are used in a group, and for lotus blossom, morphological analysis, and many other group techniques. These techniques all approach the way in which you formulate the problem and arrange the solutions in different ways, but depend on brainstorming to generate solutions.

The Group: The brainstorming process involves a group of six to twelve people, a leader/facilitator and a secretary, all involved in open generation of ideas about a given topic. The group needs to have at least six people in order to generate enough ideas, but fewer than thirteen because it may be difficult to absorb a large number of ideas and because larger groups tend to intimidate some people, thereby potentially restricting the flow of ideas. Groups may be formed from similar or different work areas or backgrounds, depending on the purpose of the group.

The Rules: There are four core rules to brainstorming:
1. No judgments are made about any suggestion. This rule is frequently broken by less experienced brainstormers, thus reducing its effectiveness.
2. All ideas, even absurd or impractical ones, are welcome. Wild ideas often lead to really practical ones.
3. Quantity of ideas is a major objective, since quantity leads to a higher probability of uncovering quality ideas. Ideas can be evaluated later. Let the ideas flow at this point.

4. Ideas may be combined, refined, and piggy-backed. A key part of brainstorming is the synergy obtained from cross-fertilization of ideas.

The Role of the Group Leader: The group leader, usually chosen prior to the session, informs the group, preferably in advance of their meeting, that a given topic will be discussed. He or she sets forth the facts, the issues, the questions involved, and the purposes of the session. Once the brainstorming session is underway, these points should be restated at the beginning of the session. The leader then writes the focal question or problem on a whiteboard or other large visible surface. (Open-ended "how" or "what" questions are advisable.) Next the leader gives the group three to five minutes to develop solutions individually if they have not already done so. Next the leader calls for volunteers to tell the group their solutions to the problem.

Once the brainstorming session opens, the leader functions primarily as a facilitator, recognizing contributors, stimulating group members to come up with new ideas, keeping the group focused on the subject at hand, and making sure the four rules of brainstorming are followed. The most important of these rules is that no criticism is allowed. *If criticism occurs while ideas are being generated, the whole point of brainstorming has been lost.* The leader too must refrain from commenting on the value of ideas, although sometimes an idea is so good, a leader cannot help but say, "Great idea."

Sometimes group members begin to tire and the flow of new ideas diminishes. At this time the leader should offer verbal encouragement or call on specific group members to suggest solutions. Another method is to give each member thirty seconds to come up with a new idea, moving around the room in some prescribed order, for example seating order, until the time allotted for the session is gone.

The same leader or a different one may lead the evaluation session. Ideas should be sorted into types and ranked according to priority. As additional research may be necessary, the group may have to convene more than once. In an evaluation session the leader must not allow the group to dismiss ideas

simply because they are unusual, but should encourage examination of far-out suggestions, perhaps by asking for different versions or ways to adapt them. Moreover, the leader should not allow ideas to be dismissed because of a lack of funds or other resources. If an idea is a good one, ways should be found to make it happen. The leader's role includes counteracting unreasonable negativity during the evaluation process.

The Secretary: The secretary records each contributor's ideas on some visible surface in front of the group. In small groups the leader and the secretary may be the same person, but it is preferable to have different people performing these functions.

Observations on the Technique: Most research on idea volume has found that brainstorming generates a much greater number of ideas than normal group problem solving, and more ideas than the same number of individuals working independently.[5] Its features of spontaneity, suspended judgment, and absence of criticism promote an increase not only in the quantity but also in the quality of new ideas.

A typical idea generation session, being very intense, should last no more than thirty to forty minutes. Experienced brainstorming groups may be able to go as long as an hour. Problem topics should be narrow, and no more than one topic should be covered in a session. For example, don't try to name a product and figure out a distribution system in thirty minutes. Individuals should be given time to "brainstorm" ideas by themselves before ideas are offered to the group openly.

Because the process appears simple, you may be tempted to discount this method. Don't. Thousands of organizations have used brainstorming successfully. You cannot imagine the synergism resulting from this method unless you try it.

Brainstorming can be used for a wide variety of problems, including not only marketing and product issues but strategy, planning, policy, organization, leadership, staffing, motivation, control, and communication. However, the process is not particularly useful with broad and complex problems.

Some of the ideas produced may be of low quality or obvious generalities. Brainstorming often produces what are called "low hanging fruit" solutions—the easy solutions. Solutions higher up on the idea tree—the more difficult ones to conceive—are often the more dominant ideas. Brainstorming is not successful in situations that require trial and error as opposed to judgment. There are no apparent rewards for group members other than the experience of participation and ownership. Group members may not see the final solution implemented and may therefore be reluctant to participate in further sessions.[6]

Software. Brainstorming software is included in a number of general creative problem solving packages.

Experiences with the Process

Many organizations use brainstorming to solve a wide variety of problems. For example, after hurricane Katrina, New Orleans government officials and business leaders brainstormed ideas for rebuilding New Orleans focusing on "changing the dynamic" that had crippled the city for much of its history;[7] and the Red Cross used brainstorming to train its volunteers to cope with the issues they would face in New Orleans in attempting to assist those who remained and those who would return to the Big Easy.[8]

And after MindShare, a global, full service media company, acquired Yahoo! as a client, its New York office developed its first media plan for one of Yahoo!'s new ventures, "Personals," using brainstorming groups from both companies. After reviewing key research findings, Yahoo!'s Buzz Marketing division and MindShare's Wow Factory brainstorming groups decided to meld online dating, reality broadcasting and outdoor advertising into an award winning campaign for Yahoo! Personals. It launched its "Project Real People" campaign by web casting 12 hours a day over three days the adventures of Julie Koehnen who, "skimmed Yahoo! Personals profiles online, had nine dates and fielded interviews from radio and TV stations— all from a billboard off Los Angeles' Sunset Strip." Project Real People later followed 50 singles over a year that used the company's Personals services.[9]

When Singapore Airlines was designing the interior space for the ten A380 jumbo jets it had ordered from Airbus, it used customer focus groups in Singapore, London, and New York to brainstorm ideas for use of the huge interiors in these airplanes. Singapore Airlines recognized that customers had largely been left out of the design of airplane space utilization with engineers and airline personnel making the decisions. The consequence of course, is that most passengers feel shoehorned into their seats. Numerous creative ideas resulted from Singapore Airlines' customers' brain-storming sessions including hot tubs, shower areas, a cocktail lounge with a view, a small gym, and even a disco.[10]

And just some of thousands of other examples include the following: thrift bank Lowell Five used brainstorming extensively in determining how to best utilize its marketing budget;[11] Boeing used brainstorming to determine the numerous types of experiments that could be done aboard the international space station;[12] and movie director Louis Leterrier ("Transporter 2") brainstormed with French colleague Gaspar Noe ("Irreversible") to conceptualize how to bring some of Noe's creative stylistic techniques to Leterrier's latest work.[13] And finally, International Paper Company (IP) opened a Packaging Innovation Center in Middletown, New York, to help its customers design the best possible packages for their products. The IP center brings customers together with IP's package designers, scientists, technicians and product specialists for brainstorming sessions.[14]

SUMMARY OF STEPS

1. Select a group consisting of six to twelve people, a leader and a recorder.
2. The leader defines the problem for the group, preferably in advance of the brainstorming session.
3. Participants are given time at the beginning of the session to individually think of solutions if they have not already done so.
4. The group suggests solutions to the problem in an interactive format, following the four rules of brainstorming:
   - No judgments are made about any suggestion.
   - All ideas, even absurd or impractical ones, are welcome.
   - Quantity of ideas is a major objective, since it leads to quality.
   - Ideas may be combined, refined, and piggybacked.

Japanese Creativity Techniques

Most Japanese creativity techniques are derived from some form of brainstorming.[15] These approaches to problem solving serve the group-oriented Japanese quite well. Western-style brainstorming, with its requirement of verbally tossing out ideas as they are thought of, does not serve the Japanese as well. Being more reserved than people of other nationalities and reluctant to dispute the opinions of others, the Japanese do not often express their thoughts openly. They have developed several variations of brainstorming, each in its own way aimed at adapting the creative power of the process to create a culturally acceptable technique.

These techniques are often used in a creativity circle, which has evolved from the more familiar quality circle. When problems cannot be solved quickly using the conventional techniques (usually quality control), the circle turns to creative processes. The creativity circle involves a work group trying to solve problems together in a creative manner. The brainstorming involved in such circles tends to be incremental in nature and focused on a particular issue. Participants would be asked to think of new ideas for solving the problem before coming to the next circle meeting. This they might do on the weekends, at home, on the train on the way home after work, or over drinks with colleagues.

発
想

Hassoo
Generating
Breakthroughs

Participants present their ideas to the circle (usually anonymously, in writing), where they are analyzed for their potential use in solving the problem at hand. If the ideas are presented verbally, the group's comments will be made after a period of time for reflection, and often after hearing some of the responses of others, with time set aside for piggybacking on those. Four Japanese variations on brainstorming are described later in this chapter: Lotus blossom technique (MY), Mitsubishi method, NHK method, and TKJ method. These techniques can be used in U.S. organizations without changing any of their components or with adjustments as the user sees fit.

CHAPTER
5

66/2. BRAINWRITING

Brainwriting is a form of non-oral brainstorming to which the basic brainstorming rules apply. Participants, sitting in a circle, write down their ideas for solving a given problem and pass their papers to their neighbors in the circle, who then brainstorm the ideas for a specified period, say five minutes, and then pass the papers on to the next person. The purpose here is to help you build on the ideas of others, to improve them. Three exchanges are usually enough to produce a lot of good ideas. The leader can then read the ideas, have them written on the board, and so on, direct the group to repeat the brainstorming exercise if necessary.[16] The principal advantage of brainwriting is that the leader is unlikely to influence participants unduly. The main disadvantage is the lack of spontaneity. I like to have the first person prepare three columns for the 1st, 2nd and 3rd person's ideas so that we can find out how the solution progressed from person to person. The first set of ideas usually takes only about two minutes and the later rounds take more time because participants have to read the other peoples' ideas before adding their own.

SUMMARY OF STEPS

1. The problem is identified.
2. Participants, sitting in a circle, write down their ideas for solving the problem.
3. After a specified period, participants pass their ideas on to the next person in the circle.
4. This person then piggybacks on the original solutions to develop new ones, writing them on the same piece of paper.
5. Three or more iterations occur.
6. Ideas are read aloud, written on a white board, or discussed and evaluated in some other way.

67/3. BRAINWRITING POOL

There are a number of variations of brainwriting developed at the Batelle Institute in Frankfurt, Germany. They include brainwriting pool, gallery method, pin card technique, and the SIL method.[17] In brainwriting pool, a group of six to eight people sitting around a table write down their ideas about a given problem. As soon as a participant has written down four ideas, that person may put his or her paper in the middle of the table. However, people are allowed to continue writing down their ideas without being obliged to pass their papers to the center. When participants run out of ideas they exchange their paper for one from the middle of the table and produce new ideas by piggybacking on the ideas listed there. Eventually all participants should exchange their paper for one of those in the brain pool. The session should go on for about half an hour.

This method gives participants freedom to continue with their own thoughts rather than forcing them to add to the thoughts of others.

SUMMARY OF STEPS

1. The problem is identified.
2. A group of six to eight people, sitting around a table, write their solutions to the problem on a piece of paper.
3. After writing down at least four ideas, each person places his or her piece of paper in the center of the table.
4. When participants run out of ideas, they may choose one of the slips of paper from the center of the table and piggyback on those ideas to create new ones.
5. Eventually every participant should exchange his or her piece of paper for one in the center of the table.

68/4. BRAINWRITING 6-3-5

Brainwriting 6-3-5 was developed by Professor Bernd Rohrbach of Bad Homburg, Germany.[18] The name of this method is derived from the fact that six people produce three new ideas in three columns within five minutes. After five minutes the paper is passed on to the next person, who adds his or her variations to these ideas. This process is repeated six times until all the participants have contributed to all the papers. Theoretically, within thirty minutes the group can produce 108 ideas; realistically, by the time you allow for duplications, perhaps sixty good ideas emerge. Still, this is a very productive effort.

You might want to modify this process so that less time is given for the first iteration and increasingly more time is given for each iteration that follows. The first set of ideas usually takes only about two minutes and the later rounds take more time because participants have to read the other peoples' ideas before adding their own.

SUMMARY OF STEPS

1. The problem is identified.
2. Six people, sitting in a circle, write down three ideas in three columns within a specified time.
3. Participants then pass their ideas on to the next person in the circle.
4. This person piggybacks on the original solutions and develops new ones, writing these beneath the solutions offered by the previous person.
5. The process is repeated until every person has contributed to every other person's original thoughts.
6. The results are discussed and evaluated.

69/5   CRAWFORD SLIP METHOD

In 1925 C. C. Crawford of the University of Southern California invented the Crawford slip method (CSM), a type of brainstorming.[19] The name is derived from the use of slips of paper, about the size of note cards, on which participants write their ideas. A CSM group may consist of any number of people, but larger groups are desirable since the time allotted for generating ideas is short—normally about ten minutes. About 400 ideas should be produced by a group of 20 people in a thirty- to forty-minute period. The process consists of four key steps.

144

STEP 1

The facilitator creates target or focus statements. These are statements that help draw responses from participants. Targets must be carefully constructed. Most idea generation methods simply state a problem. In CSM, a problem area related to an issue is identified and an overall problem is stated. Then additional statements are made that further define the problem. Two representative target statements are shown in Tables 5.1 and 5.2.

STEP 2

Participants then write their replies on slips of paper, using one slip for each idea. The slips are small (4 1/4 by 2 3/4 inches) to ensure that answers are concise and clearly written. (This size also helps ease data reduction in later steps of the process.) (Note cards will suffice.)

In writing their responses, participants follow specific rules:
- Write across the long edge, not across the end of the slip.
- Write on the very top edge of the slip.
- Write only one sentence per slip.
- Use a new slip for explanations.
- Avoid words like "it" or "this."
- Write out acronyms the first time they are used.
- Write short sentences using simple words.
- Write for people outside your field.
- Write until time is called.

Participants are then thanked for their inputs and usually dismissed. In most cases participants do not take part in the data reduction process. (CSM is similar to the TKJ method described later in this chapter except that in the TKJ method participants help in the data reduction process.) Participants are, however, given a summary of the results.

TABLE 5.1 Target A

TQM Implementation Problems: (Problem Area)
Where is the System Lacking? (Overall Problem)

- What is less than perfect in the way TQM is implemented?

- What difficulties do you and your colleagues have in implementing TQM?

- What are the roadblocks, bottlenecks, delays, and frustrations you have experienced while implementing TQM?

- Write each trouble, failure, waste, fraud, or abuse related to TQM implementation on a separate slip.

Source: Janet Fiero, "The Crawford Slip Method," *Quality Progress* (May 1992), pp. 40, 41.

TABLE 5.2 Target B

Advice to Decision Makers: (Problem Area)
How to Implement TQM? (Overall Problem)

- Remedies are the flip side of problems

- Provide your best recommendations for eliminating or alleviating the troubles you just identified.

- What different policies, approaches, or procedures have you used or seen used that worked well?

- If you had complete control, how would you change things for the better?

- Write any first ideas on a slip—don't wait for the optimum solution

- Write each remedy for implementing TQM on a separate slip.

Source: Janet Fiero, "The Crawford Slip Method," *Quality Progress* (May 1992), pp. 40, 41.

STEP 3

The facilitator performs data reduction, which consists of the following steps:

1. Sort the slips into many general categories.
2. Consolidate these into a few major categories.
3. Refine these categories and develop an outline for the written report.
4. Compile into chapters, divisions, sections, and paragraphs and edit the written report.

For the Implementing TQM target discussed earlier, four general categories, each with two to four subcategories, emerged: ready, set, go, oops. The subcategories for "go" were training, systems changes, participation, resources.

STEP 4

In writing the final report, all of the related comments on slips are itemized under the relevant subcategory headings. Duplications should be eliminated.

CSM has been used extensively in consulting seminars and projects as well as in total quality management programs for numerous companies and governmental units.

CSM is similar to other techniques involving slips of paper or 3 by 5 cards: the TKJ method and the NHK method (described later in this chapter), the idea bits and racking method, and the 7 x 7 method (both described in Chapter 4). Various procedures for sorting, collecting, revising inputs, and so forth could be adapted to the method. For example, you might want to add a visual presentation stage in which participants piggyback on the ideas. You might also want to use cards as starting points for a brainwriting session.

SUMMARY OF STEPS

1. The facilitator creates target or focus statements.
2. Participants write replies to these targets on slips of paper, one idea per slip.
3. The facilitator performs data reduction.
4. The final report is written. It includes all the related comments from the idea slips, itemized under the relevant subcategory headings.

70/6. CREATIVE IMAGING

This technique is often used in creativity and innovation programs. It is based on the assumption that developing visualization skills improves creativity.[20]

Creative imaging consists of three steps: envisioning a specific need for change, envisioning a better way, and formulating a vision-based plan of action. The exercise can be done by individuals and the resulting images provided to the group, or it can be guided by a leader/facilitator in a group setting. The size of the group is best limited to six or eight people, although more can be accommodated. A typical use of the process is to ask a group of corporate participants to describe where they "see" the corporation ten years from now in an ideal world. Since the key to successful use of the technique is to get the members of a group to respond to their visions, facilitation skills are especially important. In order to inspire group members to feel free to let their imaginations run wild, the facilitator must encourage them to shed their inhibitions.

71/7. CREATIVE LEAPS

Creative imaging is one of four techniques that are collectively known as creative leaps.[21] The creative leap is a powerful method for developing breakthrough concepts. It occurs when the group jumps to idealistic solutions, then moves back in time to prepare a plan to make them happen, solving problematic issues as it goes. There are four primary ways in which a company or group can train itself to take creative leaps:

1. Creating a description of what it wants the company to be like in the future.
2. Creating a description of the ideal competitor in the future.
3. Visualizing the ideal products of the future, those that could be created if there were no technical or financial constraints.
4. Determining the information the company needs to win.

The limitations described in the section on creative imaging apply. The facilitator needs to be skilled in unleashing imagination in a group situation.

72/8. DELPHI

The traditional Delphi process used in scenario forecasting can be employed in generating alternatives in much the same manner as individual brainstorming.[22] In the Delphi process a questionnaire, based on some perception of a situation, is mailed or otherwise communicated to experts in the field. Their individual responses are collected, and summarized, and the summaries are returned to each expert with instructions to revise his or her responses as necessary. The process continues through a series of iterations until a general consensus is reached. Participants whose responses deviate widely from those of the other participants are required to submit justifications for the disparity. These too are summarized and distributed to the others.

The Delphi technique is especially useful in situations in which it is important to separate the ideas of individuals from those of others yet to collect them into a combined set produced by an "expert" group. It is a non-interactive group technique by design, but interaction does in fact occur. Thousands of major Delphi studies have been carried out in many disciplines and in various societies. For example, the technique has been used to identify the ten most important issues of the next decade in human resources management,[23] future trends in logistics management,[24] and the expected levels of tourism in Singapore.[25]

This is an excellent technique for pooling the ideas of geographically separated experts. All participants have an equal chance to make a contribution, and the ideas are judged on their merits, not on their sources. Moreover, ideas are not influenced by individual or group persuasion. There are some disadvantages, however. The process is time consuming and requires a high degree of motivation over a long period. It lacks the immediate piggybacking effect and spontaneity of brainstorming and other interactive group processes, affording no chance for verbal clarification of meanings. Success depends on the analyst's ability to make creative use of the results of his or her study, to facilitate the creativity of expert participants, and to write questionnaires.

73/9. EXCURSION

The excursion technique was originally introduced as part of synectics, a process described later in this chapter. However, it can and should be used by itself. The excursion technique is especially useful when the group has not arrived at a solution to a problem even after using other creative processes such as brainstorming or storyboarding. It can be used for either narrowly defined or complex problems, but it probably works best on a more narrowly defined problem for which a conceptual breakthrough is needed. It has been slightly modified here from its original description so as to make it more functional.

The Process

There are four major steps in the excursion process: the excursion itself, the drawing of analogies between the problem and the events in the excursion, the analysis of these analogies to see what creative understanding or solutions can occur, and the sharing of experiences with the group.

1. The Excursion. The leader instructs each member of the group to take an imagined excursion into or through some physical location that has nothing to do with the problem at hand. Normally the leader asks participants to close their eyes and use their imagination for this journey, which may be through a museum, a jungle, a city, or any other kind of place, real or imagined. For example, a Star Trek journey through space and to unknown planets is popular with some problem solvers.[26] The ability to let go and create visual images is critical to the success of this part of the exercise. If the leader is not confident that all members of the group have this ability, he or she might offer some brief instruction and encourage people to give their imagination free rein. Participants are asked to write down what they see during their excursion. The excursion itself need not last more than five or ten minutes, but it is important for participants to record detailed descriptions of what they see. I recommend that they draw three columns on their papers and write what they saw on their excursion in the first column. If they prefer, group members can record as they go rather than after the excursion is finished.

2. Drawing Analogies. When the excursion period is over, the leader asks participants to take ten to fifteen minutes to draw analogies between what they saw during the excursion and the problem as defined. Participants are not limited to analogies; they can express the relationships between their visual images and the problem in other ways if they wish. They write their analogies or other relationships in the second column opposite each of the items they saw. Participants often find this phase of the process difficult and will need reassurance that they can find analogies or relationships.

3. Evaluating and Understanding. Now the leader asks the participants to determine what the relationships identified in step 2 really mean in terms of the problem, that is, thinking about how these relationships can be used to suggest solutions to the problem. This is the really challenging part of the process. It requires intuition, insight, and quite often, luck. Participants write their solutions in the third column of their paper.

4. Sharing Experiences. Participants are asked to share their excursions, analogies, understandings, and solutions with the

A member of a group of bank personnel officers who were experiencing conflicts with other departments described part of her excursion through a natural history museum as follows: "I saw Indians making war on another village. The analogy is obvious. We are at war with the other departments. This tells me just how serious our problem is. I never quite realized it, but, in a way, we are at war and serious measures must be taken to end this feuding before somebody gets killed." Another member of the group found her tour taking her past the section of the museum where rock formations were shown. The various layers of hard and soft rock meant essentially the same thing to her that the Indian warfare had meant to the other woman. When asked how to solve the problem, she said, "We have to take some dynamite (i.e., strong measures) to blow up the hard rock layers separating the departments."

Other analogies are less obvious. One facilitator had worked with NASA personnel for some time to develop a satisfactory device for fastening a space suit. After trying several standard techniques for generating ideas, he had group members take an imaginary excursion through a jungle. One man described his experience as "being clawed at by weeds, trees, and bushes." While describing his experience, he clutched his hands together with his fingers interlaced. While he himself had not made much of his analogy, when the group discussed it they commented on the clutching of his hands. This suggested the overlapping clutching of a Velcro strip and eventually led to the utilization of a Velcro-like fastener for the spacesuit.[27]

Observations on the Technique

The excursion technique is especially useful for a problem that has proved abnormally difficult to solve or calls for really unique solutions as, for example, in developing an advertising campaign or creating product differentiation features or unique product or service designs in a mature market. The leader needs to encourage participants to let go and to share their experiences. When the process is well explained and understood and participants are properly motivated, really good ideas should emerge.

1. The leader instructs participants to visualize an excursion into or through some physical location that has nothing to do with the problem at hand.
2. Participants draw analogies between what they saw and the problem.
3. The leader asks participants to determine what the analogies they drew in step 2 suggest in terms of solving the problem.
4. Participants share their experiences and solutions.

74/10. GALLERY METHOD

This is another of the techniques developed at the Batelle Institute in Frankfurt, Germany. In this method instead of the ideas changing places, the idea generators change places. The gallery concept receives its name from the fact that each member of a group takes a different work area and creates a "gallery" of ideas for others to view.[28] The ideas are presented on flip charts or white board surfaces. After a half hour or so the group members tour each other's galleries and take notes. Participants should not know who worked where. Five minutes are allowed for viewing each gallery and taking notes. Participants then return to their own work areas and add to their lists. The ideas can be summarized later. A variation of this technique, known as the idea-gallery, allows members to roam from place to place at will, adding their ideas to those displayed.[29] Another variation might be to use a PC or Mac and project a gallery on a screen with pictures changing periodically.

75/11. GORDON/LITTLE TECHNIQUE

This technique was designed by William Gordon at the Arthur D. Little consulting firm.[30] It was specifically designed to address the difficulties some people have in coping with abstract concepts. When problem solvers are too close to the problem to see the forest for the trees, they can only think of trite and obvious solutions, and fail to suggest creative ideas. And while several other techniques in this book can be used to overcome that problem, especially those that use associations, this technique is especially effective at bringing problem solvers "out of the woods."

The leader/facilitator describes the problem to the participants in decreasing levels of abstraction. Solutions are given at each level. As the description becomes more concrete and less abstract, more specific solutions, but not necessarily better ones, emerge. The solutions from the earlier levels of abstraction can be used to trigger new solutions as the problem becomes more concrete.

Suppose that the problem is how to eliminate personnel through staff reduction. The first level of abstraction might be "How can we make more money?" A second level of abstraction might be "How can we cut costs?" A third level might be "What options are available in cutting costs of personnel?" This technique requires a strong, flexible leader who can encourage and motivate members of a group to broaden their perspectives and think big.

76.12. IDEA BOARD

The idea board is an ongoing problem-solving exercise in which a problem is displayed on a board or wall where members of a group may add thoughts written on note cards.[31] They may also rearrange the cards, provide columnar headings as necessary, and contribute through spontaneous or formally arranged group discussion. One person is responsible for writing problems on the board for members to respond to, keeping the idea cards orderly, and establishing a time deadline. The ideas collected in this way are summarized, and feedback is given to all involved. Non-group members may be allowed to contribute.

This is a useful mechanism if the problem isn't particularly pressing. It has the advantage of getting everyone involved and having a proprietary interest in the solutions that emerge.

77/13. IDEA TRIGGERS

Props or idea triggers are extremely useful for generating ideas. Give participants something tangible to work with that is somehow related to the problem. For example, when product development consultant Steve Kange was hired to help problem solvers invent new flavors of Life Savers, he gave them a list of 75 Baskin-Robbins ice cream flavors, samples of exotic fruits (kiwis, kumquats) and samples of perfumes. The result—the problem solvers came up with Life Savers' very successful "Fruit Juicers" line.[32]

78/14. INNOVATION COMMITTEE

In this technique, managers, technical representatives, and other employees meet periodically to solve problems.[33] Employees bid for the job of coordinator by submitting proposals. The idea is that the better the proposal the more committed the employee, and the more committed the employee the more will get done. Intuit, the microcomputer software firm that makes Quicken, a program that allows consumers and small businesses to write checks and keep track of them on a personal computer, uses the innovation ideas committee to improve productivity and products.

79/15. INTERCOMPANY INNOVATION GROUPS

In the intercompany innovation group, top executives from various companies, led by an innovation consultant, meet for the purpose of solving company problems in innovative ways.[34] Other activities of the group may include seminars, study trips to other organizations, and forecasting trends in major environmental factors. Such groups are quite popular in Europe, especially Norway and Denmark, and are becoming more common in the United States.

80/16 LION'S DEN

The Lion's Den is a lambs versus the lions group problem solving session.[35] At the beginning of a normal meeting of a department, or a meeting among departments, the work group designated to present a problem, the lambs, makes its pitch to the other members of the group, the lions. Groups rotate into the lamb position periodically and are given at least a week to prepare a problem statement, phrased as "How can we ...?" The problem is drawn as a picture on a flipchart or white board. The lions have the right to refuse the problem as too frivolous, in which case the lambs must work another week on a new problem. The lambs are given five minutes to describe the solutions they propose. The lions then offer feedback, additional solutions, and so on for twenty minutes.

81/17. LOTUS BLOSSOM TECHNIQUE, OR THE MY (MATSUMURA YASUO) METHOD

Yasuo Matsumura, president of Clover Management Research in Chiba City, Japan, developed this technique drawing upon the metaphor of a lotus blossom.[36] The petals of a lotus blossom cluster around a central core and spread out from that point. The lotus blossom creativity technique begins with placing an idea, problem, issue, theme, etc. in the center cell of a three by three matrix. The eight cells that surround this center cell are like the petals of a lotus blossom. Solutions, ideas, derivative uses, expansions of themes and so on that are related to the central idea then go into these "petals." After one iteration of this process, the derived ideas in the cells surrounding the core may in turn become the centers of new sets of lotus blossoms. The process goes like this:

1.　　A central theme, idea, problem, issue, etc., is written in the center of the MY lotus blossom diagram. (See Figure 5.1.— modified slightly from the original model.)

2.　　Participants are then asked to think of related ideas or applications or solutions, issues, and so forth. These ideas are then written into the cells located in the center of the diagram and surrounding the central theme (labeled A through H in Figure 5.1).

3.　　These ideas then become the basis for generating additional lotus diagrams. For example, A would have a set of eight boxes surrounding it. So would B, C, and so on.

This method serves the Japanese culture well, especially when it comes to generating new applications of existing technologies or products, something the Japanese excel at.

An example of how this technique might be used follows: Assuming that the central theme is superconductivity and the issue is commercial applications, then items to go into cells A through H might include magnetic levitation trains, energy storage, electrical transmission, computer board wiring, and so on. If electrical transmission was written in cell A, it would also be the core theme for the new lotus blossom immediately above the original lotus blossom and immediately above cell A. Participants would then be asked to think of eight applications of superconductivity in electrical transmission, and these would then be written in the eight boxes, labeled 1 through 8, that

surround the lotus blossom A. The process can then be repli-
cated using each of the seven remaining items, B through H.

I have found this technique to be very useful for determining
uses for new technologies, creating future scenarios, and for
general problem solving. Participants like the way ideas flow
rapidly from one set of boxes to another, from one lotus petal
to another. This technique combines the free flow of the mind
map, described in Chapter 4, with the structure of the
storyboard, described later in this chapter.

Figure 5.1 Lotus Blossum

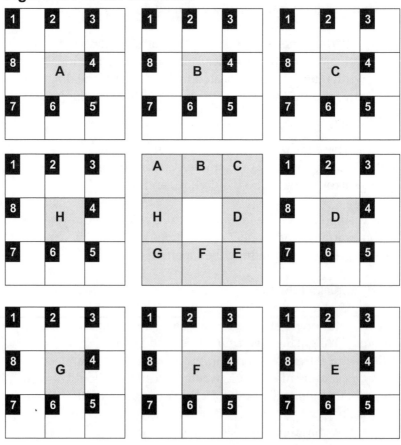

82/18 MITSUBISHI BRAINSTORMING METHOD

Sadami Aoki of Mitsubishi Resin has developed a Japanese alternative to traditional Western-style brainstorming.[37] It follows these steps:

1. Participants are given a chance to warm up by writing down their ideas before sharing them with others. This step may take fifteen minutes or longer.

2. Each participant is asked to read his or her ideas aloud, volunteering to do so as he or she chooses. Participants are encouraged to write down new ideas that build on the ideas of others that have been read aloud. Participants who didn't have very many original ideas at first can wait and read aloud their piggybacked ideas along with their original ones.

   This reading aloud is similar to what occurs in the U.S.-developed nominal group technique described later. And it has become part of the Mitsubishi method for essentially the same reason that it was incorporated into the nominal group technique: to keep aggressive personalities from dominating a session. But there are important differences, as you will note after you have compared it to the nominal group technique.

3. For the next hour or longer, participants explain their ideas in detail to the group. A group leader creates an "idea map" on a large writing surface, detailing the inputs of the group. This allows all to comprehend visually the ideas presented and, in most cases, their interrelationships. The Japanese appear to be much more visually oriented than their U.S. counterparts, and this has helped them improve their creativity. *Most authors on creativity agree that members of U.S. organizations need to improve their visualization skills in order to become more creative.*

4. Analysis of inputs proceeds from this point with appropriate attention to the cultural environment. In Japan, this means that comments must be phrased so as to allow others to "save face."

SUMMARY OF STEPS

1. The problem is identified.
2. Participants write down their solutions.
3. Participants read their ideas aloud.
4. Those with no or only a few original ideas can read piggybacked ideas as well as their own.
5. Ideas are explained aloud and in detail.
6. An idea map is drawn.
7. Ideas are discussed and evaluated in a face-saving manner.

83/19. MORPHOLOGICAL ANALYSIS

Morphological analysis was developed by Fritz Zwicky. As you can see in Figure 5.2, it involves a matrix. On a two-dimensional axis, the vertical axis might list particular characteristics, adjectives, adverbs, prepositions, and the like. On the horizontal axis would appear another set of objectives, characteristics, factors, adjectives, adverbs, verbs, and so on. The purpose of the analysis is to force one set of characteristics and words against another to create new ideas, not unlike what occurs with SCAMPER described in Chapter 4. Typically, problem characteristics may be listed on one of the axes and a verbal, prepositional, or relational checklist on the other. But any number of factors may be placed on either axis. The important point is to choose factors that may provide new insights into the problem, object, or other focus of the problem-solving effort. Morphological analysis may also employ a three-dimensional matrix in which a third set of factors can be used as occurs in Figure 5.2.

Figure 5.2 Morphological Analysis

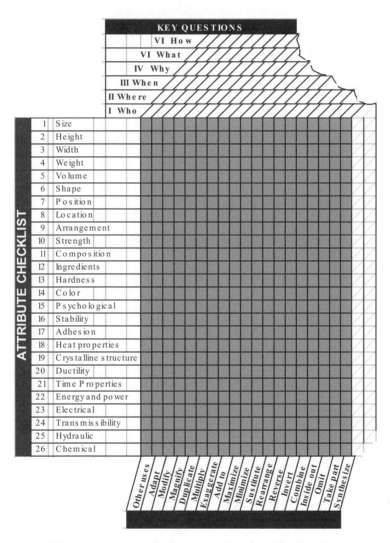

Source: Carl E.Gregory, *The Management of Intelligence*, (New York: McGraw-Hill, 1967), p. 201.

The advantage of morphological analysis is that numerous ideas can be generated in a short period. A 10 x 10 matrix (two dimensional) yields 100 ideas. A 10 x 10 x 10 matrix (three dimensional) yields 1000 ideas. The process is usually done in groups, but it may be done individually first and then developed into a pooled matrix by a leader who incorporates individual inputs. Alternatively, the group may brainstorm the analysis together. Or, the process may be done individually without the involve-ment of a group.[38]

SUMMARY OF STEPS

1. The product or service to be modified is chosen.
2. A two- or three-dimensional matrix is created, with one axis consisting of characteristics or attributes of the product or service, the other of change words such as verbs, adjectives, or adverbs. A third axis would contain additional change words, characteristics, or other relevant factors.
3. The change words are applied to the characteristics.
4. The results are discussed and evaluated.

Attributional Morphology

You can list the attributes of a particular object or problem on both axes of a matrix. The resulting cells will be interconnections between the various attributes. Three-D attribute morphology involves listing the attributes on three axes. An exhaustive list of possible combinations will result. The purpose is to generate new types of attributes by using the attributes themselves to trigger thought. As with the other processes described in this book, you want first quantity, then quality. After generating ideas, you reexamine and evaluate the product.

84/20. NHK METHOD

Hiroshi Takahashi developed the NHK method after years of training television production managers at Japan Broadcasting Company (NHK).[39] While it is a lengthy process, it acts like an egg beater, causing ideas to be continually merged and separated, thereby generating new ideas.

1. In response to a problem statement, participants write down five ideas on separate cards.
2. Participants meet in groups of five. Each person explains his or her ideas to the other members of the group. Other members of the group write down any new ideas that come to mind on separate cards.
3. The cards are collected and sorted into groups by theme.
4. New groups of two or three people are formed. Each group takes one or more of the sorted groups of cards and brainstorms for new ideas related to those on the cards. This lasts for up to half an hour. The new ideas are also written on cards.
5. At the end of this session each group organizes its cards by theme and announces the ideas to the rest of the group. All ideas are written on a large surface by a leader or recorder.
6. Participants are formed into groups of ten and all the ideas on the writing surface are brainstormed, one idea at a time.

85/21. NOMINAL GROUP TECHNIQUE

The nominal group technique (NGT) is a structured small-group process for generating ideas.[40] It can be used to diminish the impact of a dominant person on the outcome of the group's idea generation process, whether the source of the dominance is formal authority or individual personality. The nominal group technique accomplishes this objective through a process that limits an individual's inputs to brief explanations and uses a secret ballot to choose among brainstormed ideas. For this technique to be effective, the participants must agree that the group's decision is binding.

"As a group decision-making process, the nominal group technique is most useful for (1) identifying the critical variables in a specific problem situation; (2) identifying key elements of a program designed to implement a particular solution to some problems; or (3) establishing priorities with regard to problems to be addressed, goals to be attained, desirable end states and so on. In all of these circumstances, it often seems beneficial to aggregate individual judgments into group decisions. However, NGT is not particularly well suited for routine group meetings that focus primarily on coordination of activities or an exchange of information. Nor is it appropriate for negotiating or bargaining situations."[41]

As with brainstorming, the NGT uses a group of six to twelve people. The leader is also the secretary and records the group's responses, at the appropriate time, on a sizable writing surface that is visible to all participants.

The process of decision making using the nominal group technique consists of four distinct steps, which can be adapted to special conditions as suggested in the following paragraphs.

Step 1: Generation of Ideas

The leader phrases the problem, stimulus question or other focal issue for the participants, and writes this on the white board or other writing surface. Group members are given a specified period, usually five to ten minutes, to write their suggested solutions on note cards. This reflective period helps avoid some of the pressure for conformity to a particular person's ideas. Yet there is still a sense of belonging and responsibility.

Step 2: Recording of Ideas

In the second step the ideas generated in step 1 are recorded, in round-robin fashion, on the board. The leader asks each person in turn for the first idea on his or her list that has not yet been presented by someone else. The process continues un-

til every participant has exhausted his or her list of items and all items have been recorded on the board. When a person's list is exhausted, he or she passes when called upon for solutions. The round robin continues until everyone passes. This process emphasizes the equality of ideas and serves to build enthusiasm. It also depersonalizes the ideas presented and helps prevent prejudging. And it helps ensure that no ideas are lost.

Step 3: Clarification of Ideas

Each idea on the list from step 2 is discussed in the order in which it was written down. Typically, the leader points to each item, asking if everyone clearly understands that item. If there are no questions, then the leader moves on to the next item. When a participant seeks clarification of an item, the presenter of the idea is given a brief period of time, normally thirty seconds to one minute, to respond. More time may be given if necessary, but the leader must make certain that these discussions are brief and that they are not used to sell the idea to the other participants. This process continues until all ideas are understood. The purpose of this step is not to reach agreement on the best choices but simply to achieve understanding of what the choices actually call for.

Step 4: Voting on Ideas

A nominal group will often list from 20 to 100 or more ideas. This list must be somehow narrowed down to the "best" choice as determined by the group. There are several ways to proceed at this point, all based on the principle of the secret ballot. The most common voting procedure is for the leader to have each participant write the five ideas he or she considers best on a 3 x 5 card, which is then passed to the leader for tabulation and announcement of scores. Normally, the five to ten "best" choices as determined by secret ballot are then voted on again to determine the one, two, or three best choices.

In both rounds of the voting process, participants rank their five choices (first iteration) and two or three choices (second iteration). In tabulating scores, the most important item should receive the highest score, the least important the lowest. You may choose to use a scale of 1 to 5, 1 to 3, or something similar. Total votes and total scores should be documented for purposes of comparison.[42]

Observations on the Technique

The nominal group technique has proven to be an effective way of preventing dominant individuals from affecting the outcome of group decision processes. The NGT is best used with rather narrowly defined problems. When the problem is more complex, or when it is difficult to arrive at a solution, interactive techniques, especially storyboarding, may be more beneficial.

Experiences with the Process

Many firms use the NGT for a variety of purposes. It has been used to identify difficulties faced by organizational development (OD) professionals in making OD part of organizational strategy,[43] in strategic planning for an integrated information system in a large firm with many divisions,[44] and in developing strategic databases.[45] When the top managers of *Incentive* magazine sponsored an NGT session to create a more formal incentive program for the magazine's editors and production staff, more than fifty ideas were generated. These were later pared down to a small list.[46]

Variations on Nominal Group

The Improved Nominal Group Technique essentially combines Delphi (explained later) with NGT. Participants' inputs are submitted in advance of the meeting. This eliminates the identification of the idea with the person submitting it, as happens in the verbal, one-at-a-time scenario used in NGT. It also can involve a change in voting procedure to allow one negative vote to block an idea.[47]

1. The problem is identified.
2. Participants are given a specified period to write down their solutions to the problem.
3. Ideas are recorded on a large surface in round-robin fashion.
4. As the process continues, participants will eventually pass as all their ideas have been written on the board.
5. The leader goes down the list of ideas, asking if any need clarification. If they do, then the introducer of the idea has 15 to 30 seconds to explain, but not sell, the idea.
6. Participants vote on the ideas by secret ballot. Usually two rounds of voting are necessary.

86/22 ONLINE BRAINSTORMING/VIRTUAL TEAMS

This chapter began with a brief commentary on the success of online brainstorming. It is important to note that depending upon who is discussing online brainstorming, the topic may include a whole range of online creative problem solving activities some of which actually involve interactive brainstorming within virtual teams; others of which are more about individual brainstorming on line and the collecting of the ideas generated by these individuals; and still others which are focused on knowledge management, especially the sharing of ideas online.[48] Basic brainstorming is at the heart of all of the idea generation systems.

There are numerous group collaboration software packages, most notably "QuickPlace" from IBM's Lotus division, "Groove" which Microsoft acquired from Groove Networks Inc. in April 2005, and the aforementioned software from Imaginatik.[49] In addition, some Internet educational packages such as Blackboard, allow online collaboration. Email systems can also be enhanced to allow online collaboration. Because of the popularity of online collaboration, these capabilities are more and more being built into the infrastructure, and it would appear that Microsoft will benefit substantially from this trend. There are also a number of software programs which collect individually brainstormed ideas. These are then evaluated by the organization. Creative Edge in Action 5.2 reviews two of the success stories of companies using Imaginatik's software. Imaginatik's software is interactive, allow-ing online partici-pants to piggyback on the ideas of others as ideas appear on their screens.

MAKING MONEY COLLABORATIVELY

CREATIVE EDGE IN ACTION 5.2

Both W. R. Grace and Georgia-Pacific use collaborative software from Imaginatik. Paul Westgate, director of Innovation at W. R. Grace, notes, "Before we started doing this in 2001, we had no systematic way of developing new ideas." Since then Grace's chemical-manu-facturing division has run 34 online campaigns to elicit new ideas from employees. A total of 2,685 ideas have been collected and these have yielded 76 new products and 67 distinct process improvements. One of the 34 campaigns was entitled, "Customers Do the Darndest Things."

One of the primary benefits of this campaign was finding out that customers were using Grace's products in ways the company had never thought of before. As a consequence of this campaign, the company has increased its annual rev-enues by $3 million from pushing its products into new markets.

How you ask employees questions turns to brainstorm turns out to be very important. "To make online brainstorming effective, ask only those specific questions to which you really want answers," advises Westgate. "Then be ready to act on them," he concludes. At Georgia-Pacific, for example, instead of asking a general question like how to cut costs, Jeremy Wren, senior operations manager asked the company's 16,000 employees how to cut the cost of the cardboard tube that goes in the center of a roll of toilet paper. Several employee suggestions which were minor in nature by themselves, when their effects were combined resulted in annual savings of $1.2 million out of a total annual cost for these tubes of $30 million. Naturally not every idea will result in substantial increase in revenues or decreases in costs. "We've gotten responses ranging from the interesting to the bizarre," observes Wren.

Source: Anne Fisher, "Get Employees to Brainstorm Online," *Fortune* (November 29, 2004), p. 72.

7/23 OPEN INNOVATION; OPEN SOURCE INNOVATION

Other sections of this book have focused primarily on ways in which to increase the creativity of organizational members. Techniques for using customers, suppliers, and other members of an organization's industry to improve a firm's creativity and innovation have also been noted. Open innovation or as it is sometimes called source innovation offers yet another way in which to augment the creativity of the organization's members.

Open source innovation was created by Alph Bingham, a former vice president for research and development for Eli Lilly. Lilly had ratcheted up its R&D spending by an average of 14% for most of the 1990s, but despite the extra billions, their product output had not increased substantially in volume. Bingham recognized that all too often a relatively minor scientific puzzle delayed the development of major new products. Historically Lilly had assigned members of its own staff to teams to solve these problems, or had hired expensive outside consultants. Bingham hit on a radical idea in 1999. Why not farm out these conundrums to the thousands of free lance scientists who were

readily available through the Internet. By offering rewards for solving these problems, Bingham reasoned that there would be no shortage of solutions. In 2001, Lilly decided to try out Bingham's idea and invested several million dollars to launch InnoCentive, a sort of Internet dating service between solution seekers and problem solvers. Open innovation was born.[50]

InnoCentive has been extremely successful. It has over 50,000 freelance researchers registered to solve problems and posts 80 to 100 problems per week for these researchers to tackle. The best solution receives a monetary reward from one of the solution seeking firm and this reward is shared with InnoCentive. InnoCentive's top clients include Eli Lilly, P&G, Dow and BASF. Another firm offering a similar service is NineSigma which counts P&G, DuPont, Kohler and McDermott International among its clients. These services have helped their clients solve several major and numerous minor technical problems. Over half of the freelance researchers are from outside the US.

Any organization wishing to use this approach can use these services or perhaps start their own. An intra-company version of this would of course be a good way for any manager/team leader to tap the ideas of numerous others.

88/24. PHILLIPS 66 (DISCUSSION 66)

The Phillips 66 method breaks a larger group down into groups of six, plus a leader and a secretary, for the purpose of brainstorming.[51] Its developer, Don Phillips, then president of Hillsdale College, Michigan, recognized that for many people situational factors such as the size of the group and the design of the meeting room, as well as early training, tend to discourage participation. When large groups are broken into smaller ones these factors are overcome, since in small groups individuals are more likely to express ideas that might be suppressed in larger groups.

In the Phillips 66 method each group focuses on a single problem, which should be well worded, concise, and clearly identified. Participants try to arrive at a decision within six minutes.

89/25. PHOTO EXCURSION

Photo excursion uses the same principles as picture simulation (see Chapter 4). Instead of using prepared pictures for stimulation, participants are required to leave the building, walk around the area with a digital or Polaroid camera, and take pictures of possible solutions or visual metaphors for the problem.[52] When the group reconvenes, ideas are shared either on the computer or by being projected by the computer onto a screen for a larger audience, or if a Polaroid snapshot, then they would be shared in small groups. These photos are then used to trigger ideas.

90/26. PIN CARD TECHNIQUE

This is another technique developed at the Batelle Institute of Frankfurt, Germany. This German adaptation of brainwriting is based on another German creativity technique known as the metaphor technique. This process is similar to the NHK method and TKJ method which are described as processes 11 and 13 in this chapter. This version of brainwriting allows for structuring of the ideas quickly.[53]

SUMMARY OF STEPS

1. A group of five to eight people sit around a table.
2. Each member writes his or her thoughts about a given problem on cards (one idea per card) using colored magic markers, a different color for each contributor.
3. All completed cards are passed in the same direction.
4. Each participant reads the cards that have been passed to him or her and passes them on to the next person if the ideas seem worthwhile. Ideas that do not appear useful are set aside.
5. The moderator sorts out the cards that make it all the way around the table.
6. These cards are sorted into categories and pinned to a large surface.

91/27. SCENARIO WRITING

Scenario writing involves analyzing information, thinking about what this information means, and then writing scenarios which describe an organization's, a company's, a product's, or an individual's potential future. After the scenarios are written, then the most important part of this exercise begins with identifying internal strengths and weaknesses relative to the scenarios envisioned, and the external threats and opportunities that may result from these scenarios. Next, strategies must be formulated to utilize strengths to overcome weaknesses, mitigate threats, and to take advantage of the opportunities revealed in these scenarios.

Creating scenarios is mostly about analyzing and interpreting information and making forecasts based on this information. Some creativity does occur in trying to forecast the future, but it is in the strategy formulation stage that the highest level of creativity should occur. Although 50 to a 100 scenarios might be identifiable for most situations, typically the four or five most likely scenarios plus the worst case scenario are the only ones for which complete scenarios are written and detailed strategies formulated.

Scenario writing is a sophisticated technique that requires considerable time and effort. It is the thinking about future possibilities and related strategies that are important. The scenarios themselves are somewhat secondary. Few managers, professionals, or other employees think they have time to think about the future, but such activity is vital to success. Scenario writing can be used in solving several types of problems but it is most often used in preparing alternative strategies for various possible future conditions as just discussed. Internally, the firm studies factors such as its technology, functional prowess, resources, capabilities, employees, and management. Externally, it examines factors such as technological changes, competitors' anticipated actions, the expected economy, and the changing nature of customer's buying practices. Figure 5.3 contains an actual set of scenarios used by Norwegian Oil.

To create scenarios, first three to seven key drivers of the company's (or other entity's) future are determined, for example, global and/or national economic conditions, changing demographics, resource availability, the social/political environment, and technological change. (Down the left hand side of Figure 5.3.) Broad future scenarios are then forecast on the basis of combinations of the likely occurrences of (typically) two of these or other key drivers. (Found across the top of Figure 5.3 — Scenarios A, B, C, and D.) Next, a matrix of the interactions of key drivers and scenarios is created. To start, for each key driver on the left side of the matrix, identify several critical factors. For example, at the intersections of key driver "Global Economic Development," and Scenarios A, B, C, and D, three key factors for this driver have been identified and their probable conditions listed. The three factors are: the structural condition of the economy, OECD growth rates, and inflation rates and exchange rates.

Figure 5.3 Sample Scenario Summary

Descriptors	SCENARIO A: The Nation's Future is Dominated by the Oil and Gas Economy	SCENARIO B: Oil and Gas Benefits Lead to Restructured National Economy
Global Economic Development	• Persistent Economic Structural Problems • OECD Growth: About 2% • Inflation Higher: Volatile Exchange Rates	• Moderate Growth, Some Progress Toward Restructuring • OECD Growth: 2.5% • Cyclical Swings in Inflation, Exchange Rates
Geopolitical Relations	• Increasing Protectionism • Slowdown/Reversal of Privatization Policies • U.S.-Western Europe Tensions Exploited by the USSR	• Growing International Trade and Cooperation • Gains for Privatization in OECD • Relaxation of East-West Tensions: Increased Trade
Energy Market Structure	• Oil Demand Growth: 1% • Gas Demand Growth: 2% • OPEC Dominance Gains • North Sea, Barents Sea Developments Pushed • COMECON Gas Available	• Oil Demand Growth: 1% • Gas Demand Growth: 2% • Increases in OPEC Power North Sea, Barents Sea Developments Pushed • COMECON Gas Expansion
Oil and Gas Industry Structure	• Strong Upstream Operations Post 1990	• More Strategic Alliances • Greater Push Downstream
National Economy	• National Will: Unsure, Drifting • Economic Restructuring: - Few Initiatives Successful - Petroleum Sector Dominant • GNP Growth: About 2.5%	• Moderately Dynamic National Will • Economic Restructuring: Balance Between Petroleum and NonPetroleum Sectors • GNP Growth: About 2.5%
Technological Change	• Incremental Development: Fragmented Disciplines • Norwegian R&D Spending: 1.5% of GNP with Oil and Gas as No. 1 Priority • Oil and Gas Technology: Focus on E&P Improvement and New Reserves	• Accelerated Progress: Integration of Disciplines • Growth of Norwegian R&D to 2% of GNP, with new Priorities • Oil and Gas Technology: Focus on New Reserves Access

174

SCENARIO C: The Country Struggles in a Depressed World	SCENARIO D: The Country is Driven Out of Oil Dependence by Global Restructuring
• Severe Economic Structural Problems, Protectionism • OECD Growth: 1.5% • Volatile Inflation (Some Deflation) and Exchange Rates	• Strong Growth, Following Restructuring Adjustments • OECD Growth: 3–3.5% • Relatively Stable Inflation and Exchange Rates
• Volatile Tension-Filled World: Growth in Protectionism, Nationalism • Emphasis on Government Controls • East-West Relations and Trade Deteriorate	• Agreements Resulting from Stable Political Relations • Flourishing of Market-Orientated Policies • COMECON Drawn more into Global Mainstream
• Oil Demand Growth: 0% • Gas Demand Growth: 1% • Struggle for OPEC to Survive • Barents Sea Development Delayed • COMECON Gas Reduced	• Oil Demand Growth: 1% • Gas Demand Growth: 3% • Loss of OPEC Power and Cohesion • North Sea, Barents Sea Development Slowed
• Mergers/Consolidations Multiply • State-Owned Companies Favored by National Policies	• Strategic Shift from Oil to Gas • Privatization of Some State-Owned Operations

• Malaise: Discouraged, Divided
• Economic Restructuring:
  - All Sectors Struggling
  - Govt. Support of Energy Sector
• GNP Growth: 1–1.5%
	• Strongly Dynamic National Will
	• Economic Restructuring:
	  - Most Initiatives Successful
	  - Gas More Important than Oil
	• GNP Growth: 2.5–3%

• Stalled Development: Restrictive, Protectionist Policies
• Norwegian R&D Spending Overall Declines but Spending on Oil and Gas R&D Constant
• Oil and Gas Technology: Focus on Productivity/Cost Control
	• Rapid Progress: Integration, Global Diffusion of Technologies
	• Norwegian R&D at 2–2.5%
	  - Focus on High-tech
	  - Restructuring
	• Oil and Gas Technology: Focus on Gas Conversion, Artificial Intelligence / Imaging

Source: Reprinted from: *Long Range Planning,* vol. 23, no.2., P.R. Stokke, W.K. Ralston, T.A. Boyce, I.H. Wilson, "Scenerio Planning for Norwegian Oil and Gas", pp. 22, Copyright 1990, with permission from Elsevier.

The probable conditions of each of these factors are then listed for each scenario. For example, at the intersection of "Global Economic Development" and Scenario A, the economy's structure is described as having persistent problems, the OECD growth rate is about 2%, and the inflation rate is higher, causing volatile exchange rates. These intersections would be completed for all factors as seen in Figure 5.3.

The four scenarios seen in this figure were created by Norwegian Oil & Gas in an attempt to understand the future need for oil and gas, and hence their need to drill for oil and gas. From these scenarios, they developed an R & D strategy for oil and gas exploration. Note how the drivers often result in the titles of the scenarios. The scenario writers identify opportunities (and threats) and determine what the company needs in the way of increased strengths and reduced weaknesses to take advantage of those opportunities. Strategies are determined on the basis of this SWOT analysis.[54] Again, it is with formulating these strategies to use strengths, overcome weaknesses, take advantage of opportunities, and mitigate threats that the greatest level of creativity needs to occur.

There are many ways of doing scenarios, but the previous discussion describes one of the most comprehensive approaches. Scenario daydreaming is an example of an alternative type of scenario planning. When little time is available, scenario daydreaming is a good choice. It proceeds in the same basic way as scenario writing (often also called scenario planning), but it seldom results in a sizable written document the way scenario writing does, and there is much less formal research than with scenario writing.[55]

Any problem situation that is changing over time lends itself to using scenarios. Southern California Edison used this technique in planning for new electric production capacity, and determining what actions to take as a result.[56]

1. Obtain and analyze relevant information.
2. Identify three to seven drivers of the firm's future.
3. Identify four or five most likely and the worst case scenarios.
4. Identify a small, general list of relevant factors for each key driver.
5. For each intersection of key driver and broad scenario determine the condition of each of the relevant factors.
6. Determine strengths, weaknesses, threats and opportunities of the organization, company, product, person or other entity relative to each scenario.
7. Formulate a creative strategy for utilizing strengths to overcome weaknesses, mitigate threats, and take advantage of opportunities.

92/28. SIL METHOD

This technique was developed at the Battelle Institute in Frankfurt, Germany. The letters SIL form an acronym in German that translates roughly as "successive integration of problem elements."[57] This technique is similar to other versions of brainwriting, many of which were also developed at Battel.

1. Each participant silently generates responses to a problem statement.
2. Two group members each read an idea aloud.
3. The other members try to combine the two ideas into one.
4. Another member reads his or her idea aloud and the other members try to combine it with the previous idea.
5. This process continues until a workable solution has been found or the deadline is reached.

93/29 STORYBOARDING

Storyboarding is a structured exercise based on brainstorming.[58] It is extremely flexible and can be readily modified. It assists in all stages of the problem solving process but especially in generating and deciding on alternatives. In contrast to basic brain-

CHAPTER
5

storming, which is best used with a narrowly defined problem, storyboarding is especially useful for solving complex problems. It can be used not only to provide solutions but also to help define the various aspects of a complex problem. A specific format for describing the problem and a specific process for solving it are provided.

Background

Walt Disney and his staff devised a forerunner of the storyboard technique in 1928. Disney wanted to achieve full animation in cartoon features, something no one had been able to accomplish previously. To do so, he produced an enormous number of drawings—thousands more than the then current state of the art required. Approximately four times as many frames per second were to be used to produce high-quality cartoon features, giving his firm a major competitive edge.

Before long, however, piles of drawings were stacked up in the small studio. It was nearly impossible to keep tabs on what had been completed and what still needed to be done. Finally, Disney decided to have his artists pin their drawings on the

walls of the studio in sequence. Thereafter anyone could know at a glance how far along any given project was. The technique saved time; scenes could be discarded with ease; fewer meetings were required. The story was told on a wall covered with a special kind of board; hence the term storyboard.

Mike Vance joined the Disney organization in the 1960s. During his tenure as head of Disney University, the company's employee development program, he and members of his staff refined the storyboard concept. They recognized that the technique had problem-solving potential beyond facilitating the layout of cartoon features. Vance left Disney in the late 1970s to consult full time with firms on the use of storyboarding. It is from his system, as modified by Jerry McNellis and to some extent by me, that the storyboarding process described here has evolved.

An Overview of the Process

Storyboarding is, as it name implies, creating a story on boards. You take your thoughts and those of others and spread them out on a large work surface as you work on a project or attempt to solve a problem. When you put ideas on storyboards, you begin to see inter-connections—you see how one idea relates to another, how all the pieces fit together.

Storyboarding follows the basic processes of brainstorming— it uses a leader, a secretary, and a group of people working openly and following the four rules of brainstorming. However, story-boarding takes brainstorming several steps further. It is more organized and deals with more complex issues. Storyboarding demands a high level of participation, but once the ideas start flowing, those involved will become immersed in the problem. They will begin to "hitchhike on," or embellish, each other's ideas.

A Storyboard on Storyboarding

A storyboard is organized in columns underneath major elements known as headers. Figures 5.4 to 5.7 step by step build a storyboard on storyboarding.

The Topic Header. Figure 5.4 portrays the first step in storyboarding: identifying the topic. At the top of the storyboard, the topic to be defined or the problem to be solved is identified. This is referred to as the topic header. Here the topic header is storyboarding. It could just as easily be "recruiting high-quality employees in a low-skill labor market" or "differentiating our product from those of our competitors."

The Purpose Header. Figure 5.5 indicates the second step in the process, establishing the purpose header and brainstorming the purposes for pursuing the topic, which are then listed beneath the purpose header. In classic storyboarding, these purposes are to be identified before any other headers are created. However, I personally no longer use the purpose header. I have found that participants get so focused on trying to match their thoughts to the purposes listed under the purpose header that their creativity is inhibited. I have not seen any diminishing of appropriate solutions from eliminating this step. To the contrary, decisions are better.

The Miscellaneous Header. Figure 5.5 also contains the miscellaneous header. The column beneath this header contains all the items that don't seem to fit in any of the other columns. Items are placed under the miscellaneous header as the rest of the columns are brainstormed. Later they may be placed under another header or may become headers themselves if enough similar items appear in the miscellaneous column. In our example there is only one subber under the miscellaneous header: background. More will be added later.

Subbers. Each item placed under a header is known as a subber. The purpose header in our example has four subbers: solving problems more effectively; raising levels of creativity; improving planning, communication, and organization; and increasing participation. Others may be added later.

The Other Headers. Figure 5.6 portrays the third step in the storyboarding process: identification of the other headers—that is, the major issues and/or solutions to the problem, other than the purpose and miscellaneous headers. Brainstorming of the major issues involved in storyboarding reveals the following headers: Major Uses of Storyboarding, Types of Storyboards, Types of Sessions for Each Storyboard, The Project Team, Materials Involved in a Storyboard, Rules for a Creative-Thinking Session, Rules for a Critical-Thinking Session, and The Role of the Leader.

At an earlier stage there might have been a column labeled "Process," with subbers such as Major Uses of Storyboards, Types of Storyboards, and Types of Storyboard Sessions. But further consideration would have shown the need for headers for each of these topics. So in Figure 5.4 headers were created for each of them. This action reveals the flexibility of storyboarding, a characteristic that has been added to the miscellaneous column in Figure 5.4. Sometimes you may question whether an idea is important enough to be a header. If in doubt, make it a header; later you can make it a subber under another header.

Brainstorming Subbers: Typically, once all of the headers are identified, then the group brainstorms the subbers for each of the headers. In practice what often happens is that groups get excited about a particular header and want to brainstorm that. That's fine. You want to keep the flow going. Similarly, the group may jump from header to header, and that too is fine as long as overall focus is maintained. Subbers in one column are not usually directly related to subbers in other columns. That is, thought processes should go down from headers not across from subber to subber. Even if you use a Purpose header, you still don't try to find solutions that relate one for one with each subber under Purpose.

Major Uses of Storyboards. Two subbers are identified: strategic and operational problem solving. Today virtually all problems are of one type or the other. There are few tactical problems left because of the time compression caused by accelerated rates of change, but they could be listed too. These problem-solving efforts can be individual, group, or organizational in nature.

Types of Storyboards. There are four principal types of storyboards: planning, ideas, organization, and communication boards. When the entire storyboard process is following, all four types of storyboards are used.

Figure 5.4 Step One of Storyboarding

STORY

Figure 5.5 Step Two of Storyboarding

STORY
Purpose

BOARDING

BOARDING

Miscellaneous

Figure 5.6 Step Three of Storyboarding

				STORY
Purpose	Major Uses	Types of Storyboards	Types of sessions in a Storyboard	The Project Team
Solve problems more effectively				
Raise levels of creativity				
Improve planning, communication				
Increase participation				

Figure 5.7 Step Four of Storyboarding

				STORY
Purpose	Major Uses	Types of Storyboards	Types of sessions in a Storyboard	The Project Team
Solve problems more effectively	Strategic problem solving	Planning	Creative thinking	5-8
Raise levels of creativity	Operational problem solving	Ideas	Critical thinking	Composition of group
Improve planning, communication		Communication who, what, when		
Increase participation		Organization how, tasks, who		

BOARDING				
Materials	The Rules for a Creative Thinking Session	The Rules for a Critical Thinking Session	Role of the Leader	Miscellaneous

BOARDING				
Materials	The Rules for a Creative Thinking Session	The Rules for a Critical Thinking Session	Role of the Leader	Miscellaneous
Wall boards	No criticism	Be objective	Choose topic, team	Background:: Disney, Mike Vance
Cards: sizes; colors; pins; tape	Quantity no quality	Be critical	Choose type of storyboard, brief team	Visual
Wide tipped markers	Piggyback ides	Attack ideas not people	Warm up, review rules	Flexible
Post It notes	The wilder the better		Topic header headers, subbers	Use symbols
Scissors, string	Quick and dirty		Conduct creative thinking	
Table			Conduct critical thinking	

The Planning Storyboard. The planning storyboard is the first stage in the overall storyboarding process. It contains all the major ideas related to solving the problem described by the topic header. It is the blueprint for the actions that follow. The storyboarding process evolves mostly from the planning board.

The Ideas Storyboard. The second step in the storyboarding process. It is an expansion of some of the ideas (hence the name) contained in the planning board. Typically, a header such as Rules for Creative Thinking, would become a topic header in an ideas board, and each of the subbers under that header in the planning board would become headers in the ideas board. Participants brainstorm the subbers for each of these headers and may add headers related to actual solutions of particular problems. Once the ideas board is complete, then the organization board is necessary.

The Organization Storyboard. Answers three questions: What are the tasks that need to be done? When do they need to begin? Who will be doing them? It takes the objectives and plans established in the planning and ideas boards and breaks them into individual and group objectives and tasks. I like to write the organization information on the planning and/or ideas boards rather than create a separate board. Your preference may vary. Once the storyboarding sessions are over, this information will need to be transcribed in a detailed format. For this an organization board is useful. Once solutions have been identified and tasks created, a communications board is used to describe how this information will be conveyed.

The Communications Storyboard. Answers these questions: Who needs to know? What do they need to know? When do they need to know it? What media are going to be used to

convey the information? This board can be completed after the tasks have been established.

Some people prefer to begin work on this board early in the creative-thinking session. I don't. You have to have the tasks established before you can communicate them. As with the organization board, I prefer to simply write on the planning and ideas boards, saving the separate report of this information for later. The beauty of storyboarding is that such flexibility is possible.

You can use planning and ideas boards in all creative-thinking projects—they are the core of the storyboard system. The extent to which you use communication and organization boards depends on the scope of the project, the size of your organization, the number of people outside the project team who need to know about the project and its progress, and the number of people who will eventually be involved in implementing the ideas.

The Types of Storyboard Sessions. There are two types of storyboard sessions: creative-thinking sessions and critical-thinking sessions. They take place for each of the four types of storyboards—planning, ideas, organization, and communication.

Rules for a Creative Thinking Session: During the creative-thinking session the objective is to come up with as many ideas and/or solutions as possible. You follow the basic brainstorming rules: Consider all ideas relevant, no matter how impractical and farfetched they may seem; the more ideas that arise, the better; no criticism is allowed at this point; hitchhike on each others' ideas and keep comments short. (There will be an evaluation session following the creativity session.) Each creative-thinking session should last no longer than an hour (ideally thirty to forty minutes) to maintain maximum interest and effectiveness. The critical-thinking session that follows can be roughly twice as long.

Rules for a Critical Thinking Session: After the planning board has been completed to the group's satisfaction, take a break. Now you're ready for a critical-thinking session. During the critical-thinking session the ideas and solutions generated in the creative-thinking session are evaluated. Now is the time to think judgmentally.

First look at a header. Ask, these questions: Will the idea work? Why is it up there? Is it necessary to our objective? Is it feasible? If the header doesn't stand up in the critical-thinking session, remove it from the board or move it to another position on the board. Then evaluate each subber under the headers (keep in mind that if a header is not valid, it does not mean that any particular subber under it won't work). If a subber no longer seems pertinent or practical, toss it out or move it. Then go on to evaluate the next header and group of subbers under it, and so on until the entire board has been appraised. Your objective is to narrow the list of ideas to something more manageable.

Additional Steps in the Process. Once you have identified all of the subbers for each header in the storyboard you are working on , the next step is to develop the next board in the sequence. If you are on a planning board, for example, your next step is a creativity session for an ideas board. If you are on an ideas board, you need to hold the creativity session for the organization board.

It is best to schedule the sessions over a few days or weeks, recognizing that people are under time constraints. On the other hand, a lengthy "grind" session sometimes works well and may be necessary if the project is a crisis situation.

The Project Team. Before you conduct a creative problem-solving session using the storyboard system, you must assemble your project team. Normally there are five to eight participants, but it is feasible to include up to twelve participants. For demonstration purposes, storyboard groups can be very large. There may be times when you'll want to put together a separate project team to work on a particular ideas board. The wider and deeper you can go for ideas, the more productivity and creativity will result.

The members of the group should be chosen carefully. They may come from various levels of the organization or from the same level. They may come from different organizations. They may even be strangers. They may have different or similar backgrounds. For example, you might ask a vice president and a foreman to join your team. You'll want to consider the balance between male and female members and include representatives of minority groups where possible. If power or authority situations might preclude active participation, participants should be drawn from the same level of the organizational hierarchy.

Role of the Leader. The group leader makes sure the team meets on time and that the work gets done. He or she may facilitate the process as well. Because the facilitator's job is so demanding, the group may elect (or the leader may appoint) different or assistant facilitators from time to time. Before starting any creative problem solving session, the leader should describe the topic to the team. The leader should be certain everyone understands the subject and why the session is being conducted.

The Role of the Secretary. The secretary records the ideas generated in the creative-thinking session and deletes them, moves them, combines them, and so on, during the critical-thinking session. It's a good idea to change secretaries at least once during a lengthy session. Secretaries should use symbols and drawings occasionally, to save time, and liven up the session, and provide visual stimulation.

Storyboarding Materials. Originally, storyboards consisted of cork wall boards covering the entire sides of several walls; note cards were tacked to this surface. Thus, in addition to a facilitator and a secretary, a tacker was also needed. Later, people began to use scotch tape to attach the cards to any wall; this procedure required a taper. Now most storyboards are created on writing surfaces such as a series of chalkboards or a series of white boards. On these it is easy to add, delete, or move ideas. I prefer to use white boards and different-colored markers to differentiate the topic header, the headers, the subbers, and the siders. You can also use different colors to distinguish each column from the rest. If you use note cards, the topic card should be 8" x 10", the headers and subbers 4" x 6" or 3" x 5" if you use Post-It-Notes. Depending on which system you use, be it pushpin cards, taped cards, Post-It-Notes, erasable wall boards or chalkboards, you'll need push pins, scissors, wide marking pens for paper or boards, chalk, and a supply of cards or Post-It-Notes. A digital (or Polaroid) camera comes in handy for taking pictures of completed boards. The obvious advantages of digital cameras are the ease of sharing, storage, and editing.

Another Example

Let's say that your creative problem-solving project is to improve productivity. The topic card would read "Improve Productivity." Then your project team would consider what they needed to do to talk about, or think about regarding this problem.

Some major considerations that might arise, to be written up on header cards, are the following: Purpose (or not), Productivity Defined, Good Examples, Causes of High Productivity, Causes of Low Productivity, Educational Theories and Resources, Major Methods, Implementation Concepts, and Miscellaneous. Remember you can have a header labeled "Purpose" or not, and you should always have one labeled "Miscellaneous." If you have a purpose header, then you should list the purpose subbers before brainstorming the other headers. Next, work with each header in depth to develop the subbers under each one.

Miscellaneous: At first we had only "background" as a subber on our storyboard about storyboarding. Now, in Figure 5.7, three more subbers have been added. Visual—One of the most important characteristics of storyboarding is its visuality. Not just the artwork which may be added, but the very fact that the words are listed so that everyone can see them and respond to them. Flexible-One reason I like this process is that it is so flexible. You don't have to follow the rules exactly. You can change the boards around easily. Symbols-The use of symbols makes it easier to be creative, because of their visuality, and because they more quickly summarize concepts than do words.

The Personal Storyboard

The personal storyboard is a form that you can use to copy information from a wall storyboard. It can be carried conveniently in a briefcase. It will come in handy if you want to work on a project when you're away from your storyboard wall. Figure 5.8 shows a sample personal storyboard form.

Suggestions for Putting Storyboarding to Work

1. To start, choose the walls you'll devote to storyboarding and acquire the necessary materials.

2. Choose your first topic or objective.

3. Organize your project team. Notify the team members of the topic and type of storyboard.

4. Choose a facilitator, writer, and pinner/taper, and initiate the first creative-thinking session. Review ground rules. Do something to warm up the participants and get them excited about the project.

5. After a break, then, hold a critical-thinking session to evaluate the ideas generated in the creative-thinking session. Begin by reviewing ground rules. Reorganize your storyboard as you proceed.

6. Follow up your planning board with an ideas storyboard. Then use an organization storyboard and, if necessary, a communications board or some version thereof.

Experiences with Storyboarding

Storyboarding is not nearly as well known or as frequently utilized as brainstorming, yet for more complex problems, I think it is the best process to use. The process has been used successfully for a wide range of complex issues from helping a museum solve raise more funds[59] to solving quality problems at a major hospital. I recently used storyboarding with a client in the print media industry to help develop new products and with another client to help design new products. And another client, a data transactions company that was seeking to become more innovative, used storyboarding to develop a management structure that encouraged and systematically approved of innovative projects.

Figure 5.8 Personal Story Board

Personal Story Board

Date _____ Topic _____

Header	Header	Header	Header	Header	Header	Header
Subber	Subber	Subber	Subber	Subber	Subber	Subber

Final Observations on Storyboarding

The beauty of this technique is that it is flexible and readily adaptable to your needs. If you don't like the exact system, change it to meet your requirements. Some changes are minor, but some may be pretty significant. In doing a seminar in Denmark recently, one participant suggested that at her company they just start brainstorming around the topic header. Then they sort out the ideas into headers and subbers, and then do more brainstorming on the identified headers. The key is to do what works for your organization, but keep the basic process.

When you begin using the storyboard process, keep it simple. As you become comfortable with the system you can expand your applications of it. However, you may need to spread storyboards over several days to maintain the group's energy levels, and several boards may be necessary to solve very complex problems. Personally, I believe it is the best group problem-solving technique for complex problems, although mind mapping also works well with groups.

If you do Internet searches for Storyboarding, most of the time you will run across the movie/video version of this technique. The verbal technique used for creative problem solving is discussed much less but there are articles and a couple of consulting firms with websites for storyboarding.

SUMMARY OF STEPS

1. A group consisting of eight to twelve people, a leader, and a recorder are selected.
2. The problem is defined and identified as the topic header at the top of the story board.
3. The purpose and miscellaneous headers are written down. The purpose header is brainstormed.(You may bypass purpose.)
4. The other headers are identified through brainstorming.
5. Each header's subtopics are identified through brainstorming.
6. After a break, the critical session occurs, using different rules from those used in the creative session.
7. Ideas, communication, and organization story boards follow, using the same steps.

94/30. SYNECTICS

Synectics is a form of group brainstorming that relies heavily on analogies and metaphors, association, and the excursion technique to help the imagination find relationships between seemingly unrelated objects, ideas, products, persons, and so on.[60] The dual purpose of this process is to learn (that is, make the strange familiar) and to innovate (that is, make the familiar strange).[61] The process usually uses seven people: a problem owner, a facilitator, and five other members.

According to its creator, William J.J. Gordon, synectics is based on three key assumptions:

1. Creativity is latent to some degree in everyone.

2. Creativity is more closely related to the emotional and non-rational than to the intellectual and rational.

3. These emotional elements can be harnessed through training and practice.[62]

Three mechanisms are used to facilitate such behavior:[63]

1. Direct analogy — finding out how the object is like other things that you are familiar with, such as biological systems.

2. Personal analogy — pretending you are the object of your study. This is role playing in its broadest sense.

3. Symbolic analogy — developing a compressed expression of the problem at hand—a key word. Then one or two analogies related to this are used to brainstorm.

One of the major differences between synectics and normal brainstorming is the addition of criticism to the process. In fact, participants are encouraged to criticize, even to be sarcastic, but only at the right time. (As some versions of the criticism process can be quite harsh, the leader's role is made more difficult by this step.) These sessions can be highly charged emotionally. Synectics seeks to harness the criticism and what feelings it evokes.[64]

At any step in the process the facilitator may interject the use of free association, analogies and metaphors, or the excursion technique. I have found that if you focus on these aspects of the process, profitable results may emerge. It is the use of these processes and criticism that distinguishes synectics from brainstorming.[65]

SUMMARY OF STEPS

1. The problem is identified. The owner of the problem defines it, beginning with "How to ..."
2. The problem is analyzed briefly. The owner of the problem describes why it is a problem, what solutions have been attempted, and the objectives for the session.
3. Goals and wishes are stated. Participants write down personal goals and wishes for the problem. These are the vague, often "wild and crazy" beginnings of solutions.
4. Group goals and wishes are listed. Once individuals have completed their lists of goals and wishes, these are listed by the facilitator on a board. A round-robin approach such as is used with the nominal group technique works well.
5. The problem owner attempts to identify a possible solution.
6. The problem owner lists three strengths and three weaknesses of the possible solution.
7. The group critiques the proposed solution.

95/31. TAKE FIVE

"Take five" is a game that goes beyond brainstorming in its use of the small group.[66] The game takes about forty minutes. "Take five" lends itself to all sorts of problem solving, from strategic planning and forecasting to construction of questionnaires.

SUMMARY OF STEPS

1. A topic is selected.
2. The leader describes it to the participants and clarifies issues if necessary.
3. Participants spend two minutes preparing lists of ideas related to the topic.
4. Dividing into teams of five, they pool their ideas to produce longer lists of items, which they rank in order of importance.
5. All the groups, meeting together, create a short list composed of the most important items from each group, limiting the total to ten.
6. These items are discussed and assessed.

96/32.TKJ METHOD

Developed in 1964, the KJ (Kawakita Jiro) method is named for its originator, Jiro Kawakita, then professor of anthropology at the Tokyo Institute of Technology.[67] The original "kami-kire ho" or "scrap paper method" was used to generate new conceptual images from raw data. In its later stages, this technique is highly visual and helps link verbal concepts with visual representations. The TKJ method builds on the KJ method and provides more steps for defining the problem. There are two parts to the TKJ process: problem definition and problem solution.

SUMMARY OF STEPS

I. Problem Definition

1. Participants are given a central theme and asked to write as many ideas about the problem as possible on 3 x 5 cards (which have replaced the original pieces of scrap paper). Ideas must be stated briefly. The point of this step is for each individual to think of as many perspectives on the problem as possible. Each participant can generate fifteen to twenty ideas in a five- to ten-minute time span.
2. The cards are collected and consensually sorted into very general categories. To accomplish this, the leader collects the cards and redistributes them so that no person has his or her own cards. TKJ encourages the use of humor in sorting the cards and discussing the ideas.
3. The leader reads one of the cards aloud.

4. Participants find cards in their stacks that contain related ideas and read these aloud. Alternatively, the leader can stack the cards as they are collected without having them read aloud. A collection of cards, which constitute a set of thoughts, is built in this way.
5. The group gives each set of cards a name that captures the essence of the thoughts represented, that is, the essence of the problem.
6. The process continues until all cards are in named sets.
7. The named sets are combined into an all-inclusive group that is named the way the other sets were. This final set represents a consensus definition of the problem. The purpose of sorting the ideas into groups is to bring new ways of thinking to old categories of issues.

II. Problem Solution

1. Participants write down possible solutions to the problem on 3 x 5 cards. These ideas may or may not be related to any that have proceeded.
2. The leader collects the cards and redistributes them as in part I. The leader then reads one idea aloud. As before, participants find cards that are related to it. These are read aloud and a named solution set emerges.
3. As before, all cards are eventually placed in named solution sets.
4. As before, an all-inclusive solution set is derived and named.

Variations: Rather than following Step 7 of Part I Problem Definition and combining sets into one overall definition, I like to use Step II for each of the named sets identified in Step 6 of Part I. I find this gives us a better handle on the problem than recombining. This approach makes TKJ similar to the storyboarding technique which wad the previous technique discussed in this chapter.

A graphical representation of the group's ideas may emerge as the leader/recorder, when soliciting the ideas, draws a conceptual picture of them on a writing surface in front of the group. New ideas are then generated and written down by participants. These may be derived from the conceptual picture itself or from a discussion of it. Eventually these ideas may also be shared.

198

Like many of the Japanese creativity techniques, the TKJ method, which is extremely popular in Japan, uses cards, visual maps, and association of thoughts to generate new ideas. Some U.S. participants feel that it is too complicated and that it restricts creativity. Others like the fact that it guarantees anonymity.

MAXIMIZING THE USE OF GROUP TECHNIQUES

Over the years I have found that there are several actions you can take to make your group creativity sessions more productive. The following list of actions is related to face to face interactive groups.

1. Be careful about how you form your creative problem solving groups, or groups of groups/teams. Cross functional groups, cross divisional groups, and a vertical slice (several authority levels) are some typical ways to form groups. Groups can also be formed with the politics of the situation in mind. And groups can be formed according to problem solving styles. There are many tests which reveal these but three stand out. All of these can be found on websites on the Internet.

    The Ned Herrmann Group has a card deck exercise which is a surrogate for the Herrmann Brain Dominance Inventory. It is also a wonderful icebreaker. This is an excellent and inexpensive way to have people think about what their brain preferences are and hence, how they prefer to solve problems. The cards come in decks of 64 cards, 16 cards for each of the four types of brain preferences. You need three or four decks for a group of 25 people.

    The Kirton Adaptor-Innovator inventory (KAI) is an excellent way of sorting brain usage preferences relative to creativity and innovation. The downside to this survey is that you have to be certified to use the survey, or hire a certified consultant. But in a corporate setting, the cost is well worth it. It is an excellent way of predicting success at continuous improvement type creativity efforts (adaptor) versus success at big bang type creativity efforts (innovator). The inventory places individuals on a continuum from adaptor to innovator. Like individuals work best together for their respective dominant brain preferences.

And of course there is the Myers-Briggs Type Inventory (MBTI) which shows thinking preferences. The MBTI examines four continuums of behavior:
- introvert-extrovert,
- sensor-intuitive,
- thinker-feeler, and
- judgmental-perceptive.

With respect to problem solving the sensor-intuitive and thinker-feeler continuums provide the most information.

2. Keep the memberships of the groups changing. To make these changes fun, in addition to the more pragmatic ways of forming groups discussed in number 1, you can use things like age, length of hair, shoe size, and so on to put various groups together within the more pragmatic formations.

3. Always give individuals a chance to brainstorm ideas by themselves before you call upon them to reveal their ideas to the group. This allows people time to be individually creative, and it also gives the others in the group something to piggyback on.

These are just some of the ways in which you can enhance the effectiveness of your creativity teams. Another way is to apply technique 28/2 Analysis of Past Solutions to the use of groups. Creative Edge in Action 5.3 examines a special team of innovators at Samsung. Studying such a team might help the teams in your organization. Keep in mind that some maybe even much of what some other organization does, especially one in another ethnic or geographic culture does may not translate into your organization's culture. But there are always bits and pieces and sometimes even substantial portions of what is done elsewhere that could be done in your organization.

SAMSUNG'S PERPETUAL CRISIS SOLVING MACHINE

Samsung's VIP center is one of the primary reasons that Samsung, in less than a decade, has become a consumer electronics juggernaut bumping Sony from the number one position in terms of sales, profits, and market capitalization. VIP stands for Value Innovation Program. "The VIP Center is best described as an invitation-only, round-the-clock assembly line for ideas and profits where Samsung's top researchers, engineers, and designers come to solve their grittiest problems." Most major new products and related processes go through the VIP Center. The Center houses any number of teams working on key products. Typically 10 to 15 teams may be working in the center at any point in time. Some of the projects last as little as a month, with some stretching to a year or more in length.

Team members come from the specialty areas related to the product. Typical objectives for a team might involve including more features but making the unit simpler to operate; producing a 25% cheaper combination fax, scanner, printer and copier; or creating a cell phone that will totally dominate the market with new features but less cost. Teams may do research on, develop, and design products; and help make the necessary execution transitions to manufacturing. Marketing may be integrated along the way. Teams range in size from 5 to 50 or more and an individual project team's size may very significantly depending on what phase of the project the team is working on. A staff of approximately 50 people supports the teams.

The Center is all about creative problem solving, but it is also all about hard work. Team members are encouraged to go home every night to be with their spouses, but that often translates into 20 hour days on site, and just as often into spending the night in the company provided dormitories. The center is never closed. One researcher describes the work week as Monday, Tuesday, Wednesday, Thursday and Friday, Friday, Friday. Tight product to market deadlines are seldom if ever extended even though more requirements may be laid on a team.

The teams in the Center rely heavily on leading edge research capabilities but do employ some creative problem solving techniques. At the top of their list is TRIZ, which is a Russian acronym for Theory of Inventive Problem Solving. TRIZ was described earlier in some detail in Chapter 4 of this book. TRIZ has become "the" CPS technique of choice. The goal at Samsung is to eventually train every researcher and engineer in TRIZ think.

CREATIVE EDGE IN ACTION 5.3

To understand how and why of what goes on at the VIP Center, one must first understand some of the company's history, and secondly how this has influenced the philosophies and strategy of the company as seen through the eyes of one of its most powerful leaders, vice-chairman Jong-Yong Yun. The primary historical event occurred in the year 1996 when Kun Hee Lee Chairman of the company realized that the company was overly dependent on one product line, vulnerable to commoditization, and not particularly very good at launching new products. So in December of that year he tapped Yun as CEO and exhorted him to, "Change everything except your spouse and children."

Yun in a short period of time diversified the company and built a product strategy based on heavy R&D investment to achieve long term competitiveness, and cost-cutting to achieve short term competitiveness. This meant being the first to market with innovative products, not entering markets unless there was a chance to be number 1, ruthlessly cutting divisions that do not grow profits, constantly refining the supply chain and decision management. The company also focused on adaptability and quality. Now you can see why the Center is so focused on innovation, low costs, and perfection.

Source: Peter Lewis, "A Perpetual Crisis Machine," *Fortune* (September 19, 2005), pp. 58-76.

A FINAL NOTE

Thirty-two techniques are described in this chapter. You may find five to ten that you feel comfortable with. But try them all, and revisit them all occasionally to avoid getting in a rut.

REFERENCES

[1] Anonymous, "IBM Sets Up First A-Pac Lotus Support Centre in Pune," *Knight Ridder Tribune* (September 21, 2005), p. 1; Larry Rullson, "CEO Says Innovation is the Key," *Knight Ridder Tribune* (September 16, 2005), p. 1; Anne Fisher, "Get Employees to Brainstorm Online," *Fortune* (November 29, 2004), p. 72.

[2] Ibid.

[3] David J. Placek, "Creativity Survey Shows Who's Doing What; How to Get Your Team on the Road to Creativity," *Marketing News* (November 6, 1989), p. 14.

[4] Alex Osborn, *Applied Imagination* (New York: Charles Scribner & Sons, 1953), pp. 297-304; also see, Robert Kerwin, "Brainstorming as a Flexible Management Tool," *Personnel Journal* (May 1983), pp. 414-418.

[5] There is some contradictory evidence. For example see, Adrian Furnham, "The Brainstorming Myth," *Business Strategy Review* (Winter 2000), pp. 21-28.

[6] "Group Techniques: Part 2, Alternatives to Brainstorming," *Small Business Report* (October 1981), p. 15

[7] Jonathan Alter, "How to Save the Big Easy," *Newsweek* (September 12, 2005), p. 53.

[8] Taryn Plumb, "Local Volunteers Learn to Help: Red Cross Trains Recovery Personnel," *Telegram and Gazette* (September 4, 2005), p. A1.

[9] Aimee Deeken, "MindShare," *Adweek* (June 21, 2004), pp. SR 34, 35.

[10] Chris Woodyard, "Frequent Fliers Brainstorm to Create a Better Cabin," *USA Today* (October 1, 2002), p. 5B.

[11] Steve Garhausen, "How Lowell Five Rebuilt Its Marketing Unit, Strategy," *American Banker* (August 9, 2005), p. 14A.

[12] Jefferson Morris, "Boeing Team Brainstorming List of ISS Exploration Experiments," *Aerospace Daily & Defense Report* (July 18, 2005), p. 4.

[13] Daniel Fienberg, "'Transporter2' Director Cuts to the Chase," *Knight Ridder Tribune Business News* (September 2, 2005), p.1.

[14] "IP Offers Creative Partnership," *Purchasing World* (August 1990), pp. 38-41.

[15] This discussion of Japanese creativity techniques and of the four techniques discussed later in the chapter are taken from: Sheridan M. Tatsuno, *Created in Japan: From Imitators to World-Class Innovators*, (New York: Harper & Row, Ballenger Division, 1990), pp. 104-115; and a summary of these as discussed in Sheridan M. Tatsuno, "Creating Breakthroughs the Japanese Way," *R&D Magazine* (February, 1990), pp. 137-142.

[16] Arthur B. VanGundy, *Creative Problem Solving* (New York: Quorum Books, 1987), pp. 131–144. The material on 6-3-5 can also be found on these pages.

[17] Horst Greschka, "Perspectives on Using Various Creativity Techniques," in Stanley S. Gryskiewicz, *Creativity Week II, 1979 Proceedings* (Greensboro, North Carolina: Center for Creative Leadership, 1979) pp. 51-55.

[18] Letter from Kathleen Gesell, Rohrbach Consulting BmbH dated 4/17/95.

[19] Most of this discussion is taken from Janet Fiero, "The Crawford Slip Method," *Quality Progress* (May 1992), pp. 40–43; also see, Robert M. Krone, "Improving Brainpower Productivity," *Journal for Quality and Participation* (December 1990), pp. 80-84.

[20] Lea Hall, "Can you Picture That?" *Training & Development Journal* (September 1990), pp. 79-81.

[21] James F. Bandrowski, "Taking Creative Leaps," *Planning Review* (January/February 1990), pp. 34-38.

[22] Ray Dull, "Delphi Forecasting: Market Research Method of the 1990s," *Marketing News* (August 29, 1988), p. 17.

[23] J. Daniel Couger, "Key Human Resource Issues in IS in the 1990s: Interviews of IS Executives Versus Human Resource Executives," *Information and Management* (April, 1988), pp 161-174.

[24] James F. Robeson, "The Future of Business Logistics: A Delphi Study Predicting

Future Trends in Business Logistics," *Journal of Business Logistics* (#2, 1988), pp. 1-14.

[25] Yeong Wee Yong, Kau Ah Keng, Tan Leng Leng, "A Delphi Forecast for the Singapore Tourism Industry: Future Scenario and Marketing Implications," *European Journal of Marketing* (November 1989), pp. 15-26.

[26] Magaly Olivero, "Get Crazy! How to Have a Break Through Idea," *Working Woman* (September 1990), p. 144.

[27] As reported in Stan S. Gryskiewicz and J.T. Shields, "Issues and Observations," (Greenville, N.C.: Center for Creative Leadership) (November 1983), p. 5.

[28] Horst Geschka, loc. cit.

[29] Ibid.

[30] Arthur B. VanGundy, *Creative Problem Solving* (New York: Quorum, 1987), p. 136.

[31] Edward Glasman, "Creative Problem Solving", *Supervisory Management*, (March, 1989) pp. 17-18.

[32] Bryan W. Mattimore, "Brainstormer's Boot Camp," *Success* (October 1991), p. 24.

[33] John Case, "Customer Service: The Last Word," *Inc.* (April 1991), pp. 89-93.

[34] Knut Holt, "Consulting in Innovation through Intercompany Study Groups," *Technovation* (July 1990), pp. 347-353.

[35] Robert Bookman, "Rousing the Creative Spirit," *Training & Development Journal* (November 1988), pp. 67–71.

[36] Sheridan M. Tatsuno, *Created in Japan*, op. cit., pp. 110-113.

[37] Sheridan M. Tatsuno, *Created in Japan*, op. cit., pp. 109-110.

[38] Carl E. Gregory, *The Management of Intelligence* (New York: McGraw-Hill, 1967), pp. 200–202.

[39] Sheridan Tatsuno, *Created in Japan*, op. cit., p. 110.

[40] Andre L. Delbecq, Andrew H. Van de Ven, and D.H. Gustafson, *Group Techniques for Program Planning* (Glenview, Ill.: Scott Foresman & Company, 1975).

[41] Don Hellriegel, John W. Slocum, Richard W. Woodman, *Organizational Behavior*, 4th ed. (St. Paul, Minnesota: West Publishing Company, 1986) p. 259.

[42] See S. Scott Sink, "Using the Nominal Group Technique Effectively," *National Productivity Review*, (Spring 1983) p. 181.

[43] Aubrey L. Mendelow and S. Jay Liebowitz, "Difficulties in Making OD a Part of Organizational Strategy," *Human Resource Planning* (1989, #4), pp. 317–329.

[44] James B. Thomas, Reuben R. McDaniel, Jr., and Michael J. Dooris, "Strategic Issue Analysis: NGT + Decision Analysis for Resolving Strategic Issues," *Journal of Applied Behavioral Science* (1989), #2, pp. 189-200.

[45] Edward J. Szewczak, "Building a Strategic Data Base," *Long Range Planning* (April 1988), pp. 97-103.

[46] "Incentive Magazine: Nominal Groups in Action," *Incentive* (November 1988, pp. 60–62.

[47] William M. Fox, "'Anonymity and Other Keys to Successful Problem Solving Meetings," *National Productivity Review* (Spring 1989), pp. 145-156; William M. Fox, "The Improved Nominal Group Technique (INGT)," *Journal of Management Development* (1989), #1, pp. 20-27.

[48] Anne Fisher, op. cit., discusses both collaboration/idea generation, and knowledge sharing; George Anders, ""Inside Job," *Fast Company* (September 2001), pp. 176-183 discusses the knowledge management side of online brainstorming offering seven steps to a better intranet for sharing ideas.

[49] ProjectLounge.com, (September 15, 2005), p.1; MyWiseOwl.com/ Groove/ software, (September 15, 2005), p.1; also search for groupware at Business.com (September 19, 2005) and you will find a listing and brief description of numerous groupware software packages. And if you search the Web for "online brainstorming" you also find a number of companies that list and/or sell, describe, etc., various online brainstorming software packages and processes. Also, if you do a search for "online brainstorming" at MyWiseOwl.com you will find a sizeable list of related software resources. Also see entrepreneur.com/article/ 0,4621,322894,00.html - Sep 17, 2005.

[50] Robert J. Allio, "Interview: The InnoCentive Model of Open Innovation," *Strategy & Leadership* (Issue 4, 2004), pp. 4-10; Paul Kaihla, "Building a Better R&D Mousetrap," *Business 2.0* (September 2003), pp. 50, 52.

[51] "Group Techniques: Part 2, Alternatives to Brainstorming," *Small Business Report* (October 1981), pp. 15-17.

[52] Bryan W. Mattimore, loc. cit.

[53] Horst Geschka, loc. cit.

[54] Paul J. H. Schoemaker and Cornelius A. J. M. van der Heijden, "Integrating Scenarios Into Strategic Planning at Royal Dutch Shell," *Planning Review* (May-June 1992), pp. 41–46

[55] Simon Majaro, *The Creative Gap* (Great Britain: Longman, 1988) pp. 202-203.

[56] Fred Mobasheri, Lowell H. Orren and Fereidoon P. Sioshansi, "Scenario Planning at Southern California Edison," *Interfaces* (September-October 1989), pp. 31–44.

[57] Horst Geschka, loc. cit.

[58] Mike Vance, "Storyboarding" from "Creativity,"a series of audio cassette tapes on creativity, taken from the accompanying booklet to the tape series (Chicago: Nightengale-Conant, 1982); Jerry McNellis, "An Experience in Creative Thinking," (New Brighton, PA: The McNellis Company, no date); and Lawrence F. Lottier, Jr., "Storyboarding Your Way to Successful Training, *Public Personnel Management* (Winter 1986), pp. 421-427.

[59] Larry Rand, "Victorville, California, Museum Endures Financial Difficulties," *Knight Ridder Tribute Business News* (June 15, 2004), p. 1.

[60] Morris I. Stein, *Stimulating Creativity: Group Procedures*, (New York: Academic Press, 1975), Chapter XV, pp. 172-221; William J.J. Gordon, *Synectics: The Development of Creative Capacity*, (New York: Collier Macmillan, 1961).

[61] William J.J. Gordon and George M. Prince, *The Operational Mechanisms of Synectics*, (Cambridge, Mass.: Synectics Incorporated, 1960), p. 2.

[62] Tom Alexander, "Synectics: Inventing by the Madness Method," *Fortune* (August, 1965), p. 168

[63] R. A. Proctor, "The Use of Metaphors to Aid the Process of Creative Problem Solving," *Personnel Review* (1989), #4, pp. 33-42.

[64] Gordon and Prince, pp. 6-12.

[65] Ibid. For a somewhat different version see: Morris I. Stein, *Stimulating Creativity: Volume 2, Group Procedures* (New York: Academic Press, 1975), pp. 196–202.

[66] Sivasailam Thiagarajan, "Take Five for Better Brainstorming," *Training & Development Journal* (February 1991), pp. 37-42.

[67] Sheridan Tatsuno, *Created in Japan*, op. cit., pp. 104-106 for the KJ method; Michael Michalko, *Thinkertoys: A Handbook of Business Creativity for the 90s* (Berkeley, CA: Ten Speed Press, 1991) pp. 308–311 for the TJK method.

68 For more ideas see: Briget Finn, "Brainstorming for Better Brainstorming," *Business 2.0* (April 2005), pp. 109-114; Noah Falstein, "Brianstorming," *Game Developer* (September 2004), p. 47; Greg Bachman, "Brainstorming Deluxe," *Training & Development* (January 2000), pp. 15-18.

CHAPTER

5

CREATIVE TECHNIQUES
FOR
CHOOSING AMONG ALTERNATIVES,
IMPLEMENTATION, AND CONTROL

You're going to take funds from my superbly managed division to start <u>that</u> hair brained scheme?

> *Richard Foster*
> *Senior partner, McKinsey & Company, comment-*
> *ing on the likely to occur political behavior as a*
> *result of a typical senior manager's reaction to*
> *funding a project in another company division.*

Once alternatives have been generated, then the process of selecting the best of these, implementing it or them, and evaluating the results of their implementation must take place. This chapter provides creativity techniques for performing all three of these CPS stages.

CHOOSING AMONG ALTERNATIVES

Choosing among alternatives is usually described as a rational process. Criteria were selected earlier, in the identification stage of the creative problem-solving process. Now the various alternatives that have been generated must be compared to those criteria and a choice must be made. (See Figure 2.2.)

Screening of ideas is carried out in two stages. In the first stage, an idea is screened for level of creativity and degree of compatibility with organizational objectives and constraints. In the second stage, the idea is screened for its potential impact. For product innovations, this would require a market analysis. For process innovations, this would require examining the impact on the organization itself, and possibly potential market benefits such as being able to reduce prices because of lower costs.

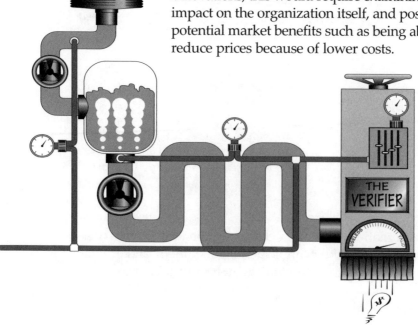

This chapter reviews two creative techniques designed specifically for use in comparing criteria to alternatives: the screening matrix for ideas and dot voting.

97/1. THE SCREENING MATRIX FOR IDEAS

Innovation consultant Simon Majaro has developed a screening matrix for ideas, an excellent way of choosing ideas that will pass the first hurdle.[1] Figure 6.1 is an example of such a matrix. Each axis represents summary criteria. The creativity axis represents idea attractiveness, which might include such qualities as originality and perceived value. The innovation axis represents the idea's compatibility with organizational objectives and constraints.[2] This might include such issues as availability of financial and human resources.

Figure 6.1 Screening Matrix for Ideas

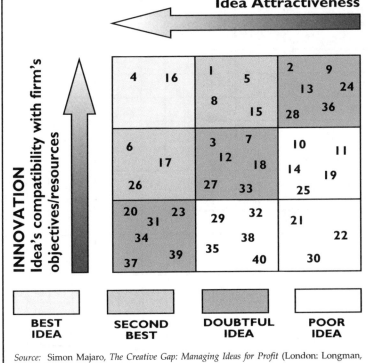

Source: Simon Majaro, *The Creative Gap: Managing Ideas for Profit* (London: Longman, 1988), p.44.

In Figure 6.1 forty ideas have been rated as high, medium, or low in creativity and high, medium, or low in innovation. The intersection of those evaluations is indicated by the idea number. For example, idea number 30 was evaluated low in both creativity and innovation. Similarly, idea number 6 was rated high in creativity and medium in innovation. This figure represents an elementary screening matrix in that an idea's position is based on an individual's estimates using the simple descriptive terms of <u>high</u>, <u>medium</u> and <u>low</u>.

To provide more accurate judgments, the idea's position in the matrix can be based on more specific criteria and an evaluation

Figure 6.2 Complex Screening Matrix for Ideas

Criteria of Evaluation (Examples only)	A Weight	B 10	9	8	7	6	5	4	3	2	1	0	AxB Score
Idea Attractiveness													
Ease of implementation	0.10												
Originality	0.15												
Protectable/sustainable	0.10												
User-friendly	0.10												
Global Acceptability	0.05												
Compatibility Criteria													
Available finance	0.20												
Provision of solution to specific problem	0.10												
Our image	0.05												
Our ability to protect (e.g. patent)	0.05												
Our marketing competence	0.10												
	1.00												
									Total score				

Source: Simon Majaro, The Creative Gap: Managing Ideas for Profit (London: Longman, 1988), p.49.

Figure 6.3

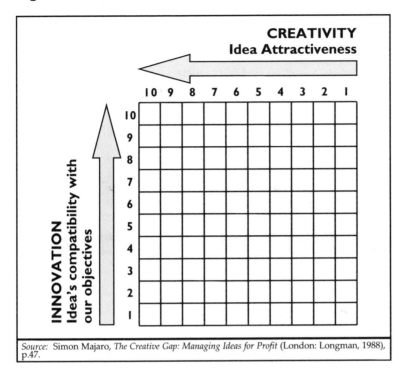

Source: Simon Majaro, *The Creative Gap: Managing Ideas for Profit* (London: Longman, 1988), p.47.

of their relevance to the situation. Such criteria are presented in Table 6.1. The relative values of an idea could be calculated using Figure 6.2. The idea would then be placed on a matrix like the one portrayed in Figure 6.3.

The second stage of the screening process can also be accomplished using a screening matrix. For a product innovation, the two axes would be the company's potential strengths (relative to this particular innovation) and the idea's market potential. Using a standard General Electric portfolio matrix approach, more specific criteria are identified in Table 6.2.[3] A process identical to that used in Figure 6.2 would result in the placement of the idea on a matrix similar to Figure 6.3.

SUMMARY OF STEPS

1. Create a standard four-cell matrix in which one axis represents creativity and the other innovation.
2. Ideas are placed on the matrix according to how well they meet established criteria as defined by the axes.

TABLE 6.1 Criteria for Idea Evaluation

Criteria of Attractiveness	Criteria of Compatibility
(Examples Only)	*(Examples Only)*
Originality	Compatibility with:
Simplicity	Available financial resources
User friendly	Available human resources
Easy to implement	Corporate image
Elegant	Ability to protect (e.g., patent)
Difficult to copy	Need to solve problem

Source: Simon Majaro, *The Creative Gap: Managing Ideas for Profit* (London: Longman, 1988), p. 46.

TABLE 6.2 Criteria for Business Unit Evaluation

Product Strength/ Competitive Position	Market Potential
(Examples Only)	*(Examples Only)*
Size	Size
Growth	Market growth, pricing
Share	Market diversity
Position	Competitive structure
Profitability	Industry profitability
Margin	Technical rate
Technology position	Social factors
Image	Environmental factors
Pollution	Legal factors
People	Human factors

98/2.DOT VOTING

Many standard ways of making choices involve voting. There are also some creative ways such as the nominal group technique. Another creative way of choosing among alternatives is dot voting. The ideas are written on a large surface such as a poster board, flip chart or white board. Participants then indicate their choices with stick-on dots.[4] Participants may have only one vote or more than one. They may or may not be allowed to vote for their own ideas.[5]

IMPLEMENTING YOUR CHOICES

Having an idea is not enough. Other members of the organization must be convinced of the merits of that idea. Selling an idea requires different behavior than creating one. You must master both creative and selling processes if your idea is to reach fruition. Implementation therefore is largely a matter of working within the organizations' culture. This chapter examines creativity techniques designed to help the manager within that context.

99/1.HOW-HOW DIAGRAM

The how-how diagram is similar to the why-why diagram described in Chapter 3.[6] It seeks to identify the steps necessary to implement a solution. Instead of asking "Why?" the problem solver(s) ask "How?" The agreed-upon solution is stated on the left side of a piece of paper, with more detailed action plans placed on the right in a decision tree format. (See Figure 6.4 for an abbreviated how-how diagram.) Each time a solution is listed, the question "How?" is asked. Problem solvers answer with Using the problem suggested in Chapter 3 for the why-why diagram as an example, the first solution mentioned is "improve product." Asking "how" results in four principal ways of improving the product: "improve packaging, improve product quality, lengthen shelf life, and shorten delivery time." For each of these the question "how" is asked, resulting in more detailed actions for each. For example, the second-level solution of improving quality consists of three more detailed actions: use cross-functional work teams during design, use six-sigma for design, use six-sigma in manufacturing. Once a diagram has been completed, the final details for all implementation plans may be agreed upon.

This is an excellent technique for forcing problem solvers to think about the details of implementation.

Figure 6.4 The How-How Diagram

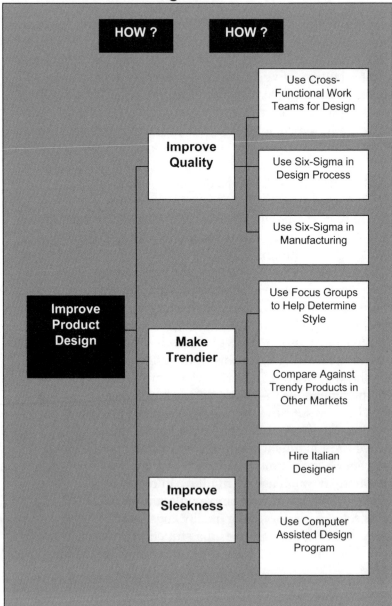

1. The agreed-upon solution to a problem is placed on the left side of a piece of paper.
2. A decision tree of more detailed action plans obtained by asking "How?" at each stage of the process is formed to the right of the solution.
3. Beginning with the first solution, each time a solution is listed, the question "How?" is asked. The responses are recorded on branches of the decision tree.
4. The question "How?" is asked again. This results in additional branches on the decision tree.
5. The process continues until sufficiently detailed implementation plans have been established.

100/2. BE A WARRIOR WHEN SELLING YOUR IDEAS

Roger von Oech, a noted creativity consultant and author, suggests that there are four distinct roles that must be filled during the creativity/innovation process: explorer, artist, judge, and warrior.[7]

"When you're searching for new information, be an **EXPLORER.**

When you're turning your resources into new ideas, be an **ARTIST.**

When you're evaluating the merits of an idea, be a **JUDGE.**

When you're carrying your idea into action, be a **WARRIOR.**"[8]

Our interest in this chapter is in the warrior role. The other roles were discussed in other chapters, although under different names and in different contexts. For example, in terms of the creative problem-solving model presented in Chapter 2, the explorer and the artist are active in analyzing the environment, recognizing a problem, identifying a problem, and generating alternatives, with the artist primarily responsible for generating alternatives. The judge is active in making assumptions and making a choice. The warrior would be active in making a choice and in implementing the creative result in the sense of getting the organization to adopt it and transform it into an innovation.

Often a person who can be an explorer and artist finds it difficult to be a judge or a warrior. Even people who can assume the first three roles often find it difficult to be a warrior. That is why many firms separate these functions, normally combining the first two in the role of the creator, and asking a group, usually made up of professional staff or managers but sometimes a creativity circle, to judge the value of the creative result. Then a manager or professional staff person may serve as the product champion, moving the product through the various stages of the approval process within the firm.[9]

Von Oech observes that the individual must move from one role to another and that this movement is difficult for many people. If you are not able to change roles readily, you must either force yourself to assume roles in which you are uncomfortable or find yourself a champion. Whether you pursue the role of warrior yourself or find a champion, the selling part of the process must be accomplished.

101/3. FORCE-FIELD ANALYSIS

Organizational development is but one type of change management. Regardless of which program is used to manage change, the manager making the changes will invariably be faced with resistance. To better manage change, the problem solver needs to understand force-field analysis, a concept developed by Kurt Lewin, a pioneer in the study of change. Lewin suggests that change results from the relative strengths of competing driving and restraining forces.[10] The driving forces push the organization toward change; the restraining forces push against change. The actual change that emerges is a consequence of the interaction of the two sets of forces. If you want change, you should push. But the natural tendency of those

216

you are pushing is to resist the change, to push back. According to Lewin, the driving forces activate the restraining forces. He suggests that decreasing the restraining forces is a more effective way of encouraging change than increasing the driving forces.

Figure 6.5 portrays the use of force-field analysis to reduce resistance to a change from using a single computer vendor, to using multiple computer vendors for the information division of a major entertainment company. This is a partial analysis of the situation as viewed by that division's managers.[11] As you can see, the managers determined that the best way to move toward the change was to reduce employee fears by providing job guarantees and training, and to provide more open communication.

Figure 6.5 Force-Field Analysis

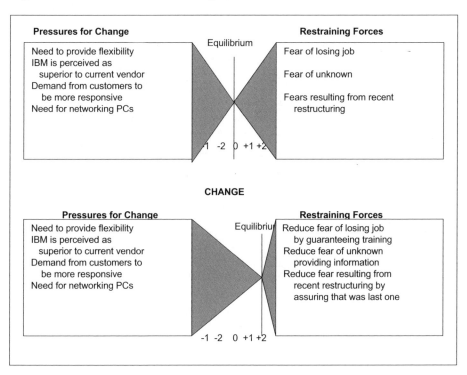

Additional Advice on Selling Your Ideas and Innovations

There are a number of approaches to selling your ideas. The How? How?, Be A Warrior, and Force-Field Analysis techniques are all helpful in this arena. One of the best processes, not really a technique, for selling ideas and innovations that I have seen can be found in a Starthrower video/DVD entitled, "Tactics of Innovation," narrated by futurist and change management expert Joel Barker.[12] Barker's theme in the video is based on the work of his mentor, James Brightman. Barker identifies five pairs of actions that innovators must take in order to have an innovation adopted. These ten actions address essentially how to overcome resistance to change and barriers to innovation. Because a picture is worth a thousand words and a video a lot more, the following verbal description can only capture the essence of Barker's message. The video provides a richer understanding than words alone can.

1. Upside Yes, Downside No.
    - Upside yes—you have to make a strong case for the upside, that is, the benefits to the audience be it a potential customer, your boss, or a bank. "Think of the money you'll save by using our new product."
    - Downside no—the downsides must be small, and in a related vein, you need to be able to handle objections raised by the downsides. "This is a perfectly safe operation. In the test trials we have experienced absolutely no problems "
2. Seemingly Simple, Small Steps.
    - Seemingly Simple—to the audience, the innovation must seem simple even if making the product or creating the process is truly difficult. Think of the cell phone with its over 200 parts but that operates with a simple menu.
    - Small Steps—change is best introduced in incremental steps so that the leap to adoption doesn't seem like a major effort. Think about how to divide the change created by the inno-

vation into a series of small steps so that it is not overwhelming.

3. Clear Message, Compatible Fit.
   - Clear Message—the pitch to the audience must be readily understandable. Make it so simple that "even a caveman can do it."
   - Compatible Fit—the innovation must fit with what the organization is already doing, or at least appear to fit. "It's just an extension of the Ideas Program."

4. Credible Messenger, Reliable Performance.
   - Credible Messenger—you or whoever you use to make your pitch to an audience must be credible, either specifically in relation to the innovation, or in general. Think of Michael Jordan selling Nike basketball shoes.
   - Reliable Performance—you must be able to demonstrate that the product or service or process has been and will be reliable. "We have tested this product with over a thousand consumers and found 99.9% successful performance."

5. Easy In, Easy Out
   - Easy In—the price must not be too high, the effort to use not to, the change required not too large. "Yours for only $199."
   - Easy Out—no one wants to be trapped in a mistake. So there has to be an easy way out. Think 30 day, money back guarantee.

Figure 6.6 Selling Others on Your Creative Ideas

				SELLING OTHERS ON	
Purpose	**Preparation**	**Who**	**How**	**Ability/ Personality**	**Style**
To effectively sell an idea.	Convince self first.	Peers.	Stress benefits.	Competitive/ comfortable.	Presentation skills.
To make myself more successful.	Provide examples of usefulness.	Boss. Subordinates.	Know needs. Show profits.	Visualize/ enthusiasm.	Know yourself. Know
To make more money for company.	Know obstacles and prepare to overcome.	Power bases. Clients.	Help reduce costs.	Learn from perseverance.	audience. Keep it in
To make more income for myself.	Gather supportive facts.	Leaders.		Cope with failure.	perspective.
To make job easier.	Seek support.			Probes.	
	Find coalition power base.				
	Know politics of situation.				
	Be able to use tools/ presentation skills.				
	Bracing people — drop hints.				

The text that relates to this figure follows on page 222.

YOUR CREATIVE IDEAS

Credibility	Costs	Culture	Results	Presentation Skills	Personality	Misc.
How to raise current level.	How much.	Innovative or not.	Long term vs. short term.	Factual.	Innovator vs. adaptor.	
Use credible descriptions.	How financed.	Receptive to creativity or not.	Quantifiable.	Big picture.	Believe in idea yourself.	
Use information to support.		Who are decision makers.	Qualitative.	Persuasive.	Persistence.	
			How will this fit into strategic plan?	Learnable.	Self-assurance.	
		How do you get to them: — politics.		Pizzazz.		
		Two-stage sales process.		Know yourself.		

As with any recommended set of actions, there are caveats. These five pairs of actions don't apply to every situation. There are, for example, some instances in which the innovation will have its downsides, or it won't fit with what the organization is already doing or the customer is already using, or it will be very expensive, or once adopted it will be costly to abandon. For example, enterprise resource planning systems which integrate all of the accounting and inventory and operations information for an organization are extremely expensive, don't fit easily what most organizations are already doing, are difficult to start and once underway are difficult and expensive to abandon. So the truth has to be laid out right up front, although the process can be divided into a series of steps which makes such adopting this innovation more palatable. Plus the perceived benefits are huge.

One of the major reasons though that individuals and organizations go ahead with such innovations is because of the potential benefits. So when all factors are considered, some may have to be balanced against others. If you think back to the Hall Competitiveness Model from Chapter 1, it enables you to factor in issues such as the upside yes—the benefits of your innovation. The greater the benefits to the customer or the organization (higher relative differentiation, lower relative costs), the more likely that the other nine of these ten actions recommended by Barker will not be so critical in the decision process. Similarly for many people and organizations, the smaller the downside risk, the more likely the innovation would be to gain acceptance. Depending upon what is critical to the organization, much could be said for any of these ten factors.

In order to account for the key factors in a situation, a storyboard or other creativity technique can offer insights into implementation actions. Figure 6.6 is a storyboard created by a group of twenty upper- and middle-level managers from a cross section of firms, industries, and functional specialties. This storyboard indicates the key issues in making a sale, that is, in being an effective champion of your creative ideas. Add to it or create your own. (This storyboard was created without reference to the ten tactics of innovation described by Joel Barker.)

ONE FINAL COMMENT

One final comment on selling your new ideas, products, or processes: don't ever forget the politics of the selling situation. There may be people just waiting to help you over the edge of the cliff.

CONTROLLING FOR PERFORMANCE

No specific techniques are presented here. Several of the approaches described in Chapter 3 are control techniques. Traditional control activities overlap with analyzing the environment and identifying and recognizing the problem. Benchmarking and best practices, for example, are control activities as well as creative ways of scanning the environment. Similarly, Camelot fulfills the conceptual model of control, that is, set standards, measure performance, compare the two, and then take the necessary corrective actions.

REFERENCES

[1] Most of this discussion is based on Simon Majaro, *The Creative Gap: Managing Ideas for Profit* (London: Longman, 1988), 44-50. I have taken his basic concept and revised it to make its use consistent with other such matrices, for example, those used in portfolio management.

[2] I have expanded Majaro's concept a bit here. He views screening as a two step process. I have combined both steps into one, and used the matrix to do both. He uses it to do only the first part of screening, that is mostly concerned with the organization's needs. I add market factors.

[3] For a discussion see James M. Higgins and Julian W. Vincze, *Strategic Management: Text and Cases*, 5th. ed. (Ft. Worth, Texas; Dryden Press, 1993), pp. 266-268

[4] Bryan W. Mattimore, "Brainstormers Boot Camp," *Success* (October 1991), p. 28.

[5] Bryan W. Mattimore, ibid.

[6] Simon Majaro, *The Creative Gap: Managing Ideas for Profit* (London: Longman, 1988), p. 153.

[7] This material is taken from Roger von Oech, *A Kick in the Seat of the Pants* (New York: Perennial Library, 1986), pp. 12-19.

[8] Ibid., p. 16.

[9] Don Frey, "Learning the Ropes: My Life as a Product Champion," *Harvard Business Review* (September-October 1991), pp. 46–56.

[10] Kurt Lewin, *Field, Theory, and Social Science: Selected Theoretical Papers* (New York: Harper & Row, 1951).

[11] Author's consultation with managers in this division.

[12] Starthrower can be found at Starthrower.com.

USING THE TECHNIQUES

Become the change you are seeking.

Mahatma Ghandi

Let me close by emphasizing the importance of consciously planning to use these techniques. These techniques are extremely helpful, but only if you use them. Read them first, then formulate a plan to use them, and then integrate them into your problem-solving efforts, those of your work group, and if possible, those of the rest of your organization. I have trained many managers who now never run a meeting without using these techniques. Many senior level and professional meetings in numerous organizations are based around these techniques. From product design and development to process redesign and service continuous improvement, these techniques will be vital to success if you will just use them.

You and the members of your team or your leader/manager will not find all of them suitable for your needs and sometimes you will not feel particularly comfortable with a technique. That is to be expected, and that is one advantage of having so many at your fingertips. Finally, don't just use a few favorites; rotate using the various techniques to keep from going down the same brainwave paths which happens when you use the same techniques over and over.

Trusting Your Intuition

Intuition can and should be used in all stages of creative problem solving. Rationality is a major contributor to the problem-solving process, but rationality alone does not result in the best solutions to many problems, especially complex problems. If rationality alone sufficed, computers would make all the decisions. As problems become more complex, the need to use intuition in problem solving becomes more critical. Research and experience indicate that complex problems almost defy rational analysis. They require the ability to see connections among numerous variables, connections that often are not discernible in the rational approach.

APPENDIX I

A Quick Guide to the Processes

	PROCESS:	BRIEF DESCRIPTION AND/OR BEST USED FOR:
STAGE: ENVIRONMENTAL ANALYSIS		
1/1	Comparisons against others: benchmarking, best practices, race against phantom competitors	Highly competitive strategic situations for finding quality/cost problems, innovative solutions
2/2	Hire futurists, consultants	When an outside view will help, when you don't have the manpower or funds for internal effort
3/3	Monitor weak signals	Identifying weak signals in the market, strategic scanning, strategic issue identification
4/4	Opportunity searches	New situations, new applications of current knowledge, strategic situations
STAGE: PROBLEM RECOGNITION		
5/1	Camelot	To make sure problems haven't been overlooked, uses an idealized situation
6/2	Checklists	Finding problem with existing products/services/operations; developing promotional ideas
7/3	Inverse brainstorming	When routine techniques haven't suggested many problems
8/4	Limericks and parodies	When straightforward approaches haven't produced many problems or insights, to add humor
9/5	Listing complaints	Looking for internal or customer problems
10/6	Responding to someone else	When someone else offers opportunities or problems
11/7	Role playing	Group, personal insights into simple and complex problems, especially good for interpersonal and customer relations problems
12/8	Suggestion programs	Systematic problem recognition when employee participation is sought
13/9	Workouts and other work group/team approaches	Complex problems where group inputs and team building are important. Workouts are best used at a retreat

227

STAGE: PROBLEM IDENTIFICATION

14/1	Bounce it off someone else	When you want to make sure you haven't overlooked anything
15/2	Consensus building	When a group definition of the problem is important
16/3	Draw a picture of the problem	Complex problems use visualization to "see" problem
17/4	Experience kit	To get people more personally involved in the issue
18/5	Fishbone diagram	Seeks better understanding of causes
19/6	"King of the mountain"	Group definition of problem, a fun activity
20/7	Redefining the problem or opportunity	Increased insight into real problem
21/8	Rewrite objectives several different ways	For different views of the problem
22/9	"Squeeze and stretch"	For understanding causes of more complex problems
23/10	What do you know?	To get started on problems
24/11	What patterns exist?	For understanding more complex problems
25/12	Why-why diagram	To better understand the causes of a complex problem

STAGE: MAKING ASSUMPTIONS

26/1	Assumption reversal	For understanding assumptions and gaining possible solutions

STAGE: ALTERNATIVE GENERATION, INDIVIDUAL BASED

27/1	Analogies and metaphors	When a new perspective is needed
28/2	Analysis of past solutions	Applying other people's solutions to your problem
29/3	Association	When new zest is needed, generates lots of ideas
30/4	Attribute association chains	Product/service changes
31/5	Attribute listing	Product/service changes

32/6	Back to the customer	For satisfying customer needs; similar to Back to the Sun
33/7	"Back to the sun"	Focused association
34/8	Circle of opportunity	Changing product or service, when a new approach is needed
35/9	Computer programs	Complex problems. Computer programs generally lead you through CPS stages, offer suggestions. Some enhance processes such as brainstorming
36/10	Deadlines	To put pressure on to increase creativity
37/11	Direct analogies	To transfer knowledge from one field to another
38/12	Establish idea sources	Find sources which can offer solutions
39/13	Examine it with the senses	New insights, complex or simple problems, focused association
40/14	FCB grid	Positioning products
41/15	Focused-object	Similar to association and forced relationship techniques
42/16	Fresh eye	When insiders are having trouble seeing the forest for the trees
43/17	Google Storming	When you really need to get new thoughts and go down different brain paths
44/18	Idea Bits and Marking	Organizing your ideas, complex problems
45/19	Input-Output	Engineering, operations management; generates a number of possible solutions
46/20	Mind mapping	Generate new ideas, identify all issues and subissues to a problem, develop intuitive capacity
47/21	Listening to music	Generating alternatives/opportunities through subconscious
48/22	Name possible uses	Generating new uses for a product
49/23	The Napoleon technique	Gaining totally new insights, when other techinques have failed
50/24	Organized random search	Simple ways to get new thoughts

51/25	Personal analogies	To get people more personally involved in the problem
52/26	Picture stimulation	Uses visualization to improve insight
53/27	Product improvement checklist (PICL)	Create new products/services, improve old ones
54/28	Relatedness	Generating lots of ideas fast, similar to association
55/29	Relational words	Artistic efforts, writing, or product name/development
56/30	Reversal—dereversal	Problems you don't seem to be making much headway on
57/31	Rolling in the Grass of Ideas	When lots of ideas, concepts are needed to produce new insights
58/32	SCAMPER	Product, service, process improvement
59/33	7 X 7 technique	Organizing your ideas, complex problems
60/34	Sleeping/dreaming on it	Complex or simple problems, generates alternatives/opportunities through subconscious
61/35	Triz	Complex business problems
62/36	Two words technique	Simple problems where new insights are needed
63/37	Visualization	When you need to "see" the problem better. Can be used with other processes. Offers new insights
64/38	What if ...	Strategic planning; complex or simple problems, scenario forecasting

STAGE: ALTERNATIVE GENERATION, GROUP BASED

65/1	Brainstorming	Generating numerous alternatives; simple problems
66/2	Brainwriting	Alternative to brainstorming
67/3	Brainwriting pool	Alternative to brainstorming
68/4	Brainwriting 6-3-5	Alternative to brainstorming

69/5	Crawford slip method	Going beyond brainstorming; complex problems
70/6	Creative imaging	Complex problems, uses visualization
71/7	Creative leap	Complex problems where major results are needed, includes imaging
72/8	Delphi technique	Complex problems to be solved by expert opinion
73/9	Excursion technique	Problems which other techniques have not solved, great for new perspectives
74/10	The gallery method	Using visuals to prompt brainstorming
75/11	The Gordon/Little technique	Good for stepping back from the problem
76/12	Idea board	Non-urgent problems, similar to gallery method without time constraints
77/13	Idea triggers	Getting people involved in the issue
78/14	Innovation committee	Complex or simple problems, like creativity circles
79/15	Intercompany innovation groups	Where other outside firms can help, popular in Europe and gaining popularity in U.S.
80/16	Lions den	Two teams, one presents problems to the other to generate solutions
81/17	The lotus blossom technique	Complex or simple problems, especially good for developing strategic scenarios
82/18	The Mitsubishi brainstorming method	Brainstorming w/mapping for complex problems
83/19	Morphological analysis	Changing product or service
84/20	The NHK method	Complex problems
85/21	Nominal group technique	Eliminating affect of dominant personality in group
86/22	Online Brainstorming	Virtual teams
87/23	Open Innovation	Troublesome problem resolution

88/24	Phillips 66	To encourage participation brainstorming by breaking larger groups into groups of six
89/25	Photo-excursion	Visual stimulation of brainstorming
90/26	Pin card technique	Alternative to brainstorming
91/27	Scenario writing	Complex problems, especially strategic planning
92/28	The SIL method	Alternative to brainstorming for complex problems
93/29	Storyboarding	Complex problems, identifying issues, generating numerous alternatives
94/30	Synectics	Complex problems, brainstorming with analogies, metaphors, excursion. Heavy on critical analysis
95/31	Take five	Going beyond brainstorming; complex problems
96/32	The TKJ method	Complex problems, uses cards, diagrams and association
STAGE: CHOICE		
97/1	Screening matrix for ideas	Choosing solutions to all types of problems
98/2	Dot voting	Choosing solutions to all types of problems
STAGE: IMPLEMENTATION		
99/1	How-how diagram	Determining necessary actions for successful implementation
100/2	Be a warrior	Getting ideas adopted in company
101/3	Force field analysis	Analyzing roadblocks to implementation
STAGE: CONTROL		
	See Environmental Analysis, Problem Recognition and Problem Identification	

INDEX

* = techniques

238

ABOUT THE AUTHOR

James M. Higgins, Ph.D., is an author, consultant, professor and entrepreneur.

101 Creative Problem Solving Techniques: The Handbook of New Ideas for Business, Revised Edition is one of three books in his trilogy on creativity and innovation. The other two books are: *Escape from the Maze: Increasing Personal and Group Creativity* and *Innovate or Evaporate: Test and Improve Your Organization's IQ—Its Innovation Quotient.* He is also the author of 6 college texts on strategy, management and human relations, and the author of numerous articles on creativity, innovation, strategy, change leadership, and emotional intelligence. His articles have appeared in such journals as *Business Horizons, Business and Society Review, Long Range Planning, Journal of Change Management, Organizational Dynamics, Strategy and Leadership, Training and Development,* and *Workforce.*

He is an experienced consultant working with firms since 1985 to increase their levels of creativity and innovation as well as to solve particular problems. Dr. Higgins has also consulted with and provided development programs for organizations since 1974 in the areas of strategic planning motivation, leadership, and change. His clients have included firms such as several divisions of Walt Disney Companies, Coca-Cola Research and Engineering Development-Atlanta, Convergys, Sun Trust Banks, Florida Info-Management Services, Catalina Marketing, Kirchman Corporation, Olsten-Kimberly Healthcare, Skopbank (Helsinki), Idea Forum (Denmark), and a number of local and regional legal and financial firms.

Dr. Higgins is the George and Harriett Cornell Professor of Innovation Management at the Crummer Graduate School of Business at Rollins College in Winter Park, Florida. He has taught at the Crummer School since 1980. His research interests focus primarily on creativity and innovation, but also include leadership and emotional intelligence.

Dr. Higgins has a number of business entrepreneurial interests including publishing, consulting, and training and development.

BOOK ORDER FORM

Customer Information: Date: _____

Name: _____

Address: _____

City/State/Zip: _____

PO#

Item #	Description	Unit Price	Qty	Price
101	*101 Creative Problem Solving Techniques: The Handbook of New Ideas for Business*	$19.95		
102	*Innovate or Evaporate: Test & Improve Your Organization's IQ: Its Innovation Quotient*	$19.95		
103	*Escape From the Maze: Increasing Personal and Group Creativity*	$19.95		

Comments:
Discounts are available for volume orders
Shipping and handling is single book orders*
Sales tax in Florida is 6%
If payment is by check, please pay in <u>U.S. dollars only</u>

Sub.	
S & H*	
Tax	
Total	

101 Creative Problem Solving Techniques and Escape From the Maze ship at approximately $4.00 in the U.S. and Canada. Innovate or Evaporate will ship at approximately $5.00 in the U.S. and Canada. Shipping to other countries will be on a cost basis. Bulk rates are quoted individually, but are usually cheaper.

THE NEW
MANAGEMENT
PUBLISHING COMPANY

1960 Forrest Road
Winter Park, Florida 32789
407-647-5344,
Fax: 407-647-5575
nmpc@AOL.com